Healing Touch
of Horses

True Stories of Courage, Hope, and the
Transformative Power of the Human/Equine Bond

Edited by A. Bronwyn Llewellyn

Adams Media
Avon, Massachusetts

Published by Adams Media
an F+W Publications Company
57 Littlefield Street
Avon, MA 02322
www.adamsmedia.com

ISBN 10: 1-59337-624-3
ISBN 13: 978-1-59337-624-6

Printed in the United States of America.

J I H G F E D C B A

Library of Congress Cataloging-in-Publication Data
The healing touch of horses: true stories of courage, hope,
and the transformative power of the human/equine bond /
edited by A. Bronwyn Llewellyn.
     p.   cm.
Includes bibliographical references and index.
ISBN-13: 978-1-59337-624-6 (alk. paper)
ISBN-10: 1-59337-624-3 (alk. paper)
1. Horses—Anecdotes. 2. Horse owners—Anecdotes. 3. Human-animal relationships—Anecdotes. I. Llewellyn, A. Bronwyn (Anita Bronwyn)

SF301.H646 2007
636.1—dc22
                                    2006028440

This publication is designed to provide accurate and authoritative information
with regard to the subject matter covered. It is sold with the understanding that
the publisher is not engaged in rendering legal, accounting, or other professional
advice. If legal advice or other expert assistance is required, the services of a com-
petent professional person should be sought.
     —From a *Declaration of Principles* jointly adopted by a Committee of the
American Bar Association and a Committee of Publishers and Associations

Many of the designations used by manufacturers and sellers to distinguish their
product are claimed as trademarks. Where those designations appear in this book
and Adams Media was aware of a trademark claim, the designations have been
printed with initial capital letters.

This book is available at quantity discounts for bulk purchases.
For information, please call 1-800-289-0963.

To my therapists

Ben, Chance, Cowboy, Dakota, Harley, Jack,
Java, Merlin, Odie, Rosie, Roxie, Rusty,
Six, Star, Teddy, Topaz, and Vinnie

Acknowledgments

For permitting me to once again indulge my decades-long love of horses, my deepest appreciation goes to Adams Media, especially Paula Munier, Andrea Norville, Laura Daly, Brendan O'Neill, Heather Barrett, Casey Ebert, Carolyn Fox, and Barbara Passero.

I am grateful to all the people at the National Center for Equine Facilitated Therapy in Woodside, California, for welcoming me into their fold as a volunteer and putting up with my endless questions about all things equine; and to all the horses at NCEFT for enduring my slavish fawning with (for the most part) good humor and equanimity.

Most especially, I am indebted to the writers who shared their heartfelt and sometimes painful stories so that others could be inspired and encouraged by their optimism, faith, and perseverance. They prove beyond question the power of horses to strengthen resolve, restore confidence, and heal the human spirit.

Contents

I watch the horse. She is running. I am whole.

As the wild wind whips against her hair, across her back, against the top line of the horizon, I know that the wind is her very heart. It carries the song of thunder and hooves into her chest and into mine. She is running to make things right inside her; she is praying up a way to heal me.

If there was any doubt for me before, I know now that I am not special to her. I am as one in her mind with the rich green grass, this dirt digging beneath her feet, the golden sun reaching too high. I am equal in her mind to the passing of the day and the distance of the night, a moon shining blue and memories of canyons with a feel rather than a color. This lack of distinction brings an equanimity—I am not anonymous, because she loves us all.

From force of habit, I call her mine. I tell people about the day I found her: every bone showing dry, ribs to count hunger on, one by one by one; hooves grown over shoes, trying to touch the earth for strength to stand; sores that wept for which her deep eyes had no tears. The people put her dirty blanket on, a saddle to rub some more, a bridle held together with bailing twine. Her head hung low. In her mind she was seeking the canyon, tired of trying to heal, ready to melt into the sun.

When I asked if we could be alone, I stood beside her in the silence of an empty arena. I couldn't look into her liquid brown eyes as I apologized for my people. "If you come with me, I promise to give you a better life," I said. I walked forward, and she walked with me, turned with me, stopped with me. I cried. I took her home.

"She's lucky to have you," people would say, with their hearts full to spilling for some reason I knew they didn't completely understand. People would cry when I told them this story, a rescue story, as if they had been in her hurt body, as if they had stood beside her in the silent arena, as if her hope for a better life was their own. That is when I knew that my horse, in truth her own horse, not mine, saw us all the same. Her pain was ours, her healing was ours; her story redeemed the teller and the listener.

As I watch the horse—now full in body and spirit—I see in the toss of her head and the brightness of her stride that she continues to heal, that she continues to heal the world. She is a running story.

In the running stories in this book, we remember that there is no step between the hurt and the hand, the lost and the left behind, the healer and the healed. We are as the waving grass and drinking sun. We are the horses that are their own beings, and the human beings whom they love as much as the pale clouds and the dim past. We are the ones who love like thunder.

I watch the horse. She is running.

I am whole.

—Dawn Prince-Hughes, Ph.D.

Idolized by young girls and romanticized in movies and books, the relationship between humans and horses is simply magic.

That magic is most evident in the healing power that horses offer. No longer simply the beasts of burden of times past, horses have become our companions, our confidantes, and our therapists. I have always loved animals, but I've found that horses touch a part of the soul that no other animal can reach. First as a client at a therapeutic riding center called SIRE, and now as a board member of that same center and the North American Riding for the Handicapped Association, I have witnessed many miracles between clients and horses. Interacting with horses can be immensely therapeutic mentally, physically, and spiritually. This interaction can help clients awaken (or re-awaken) abilities that alleviate mental disorders, learning disabilities, hearing or visual impairments, or the dislocation felt by spiritual or life transitions. Horses also provide a very effective form of therapy for those who are "differently abled" from cerebral palsy, Down syndrome, paraplegia, spina bifida, or strokes.

Human reaction to trauma varies from fear to feelings of denial, anger, mistrust, or failure. Time and time again, an association with horses has been used to address and ameliorate physical, emotional, or spiritual needs. As my own experience attests, not only can riding improve the body physically, but it can reawaken the spirit as well. My self-confidence and sense of well-being improved every time I got on a horse. Sir Winston Churchill knew this feeling, too, when he wrote, "No hour of life is lost that is spent in the saddle."

Begin your own healing journey with this collection of heart-warming stories full of inspiration and hope. These courageous people and their wonderful companions prove that time—and a compassionate horse—can improve almost any situation, no matter how dire. Perhaps you will also be inspired to find a "horse healer" of your own, no matter whether you buy one, borrow one, or volunteer at a therapeutic riding center in your area. Then I know that you, too, will experience the enriching, magical healing power of horses for yourself.

—Cynthia Ruiz

The Rat

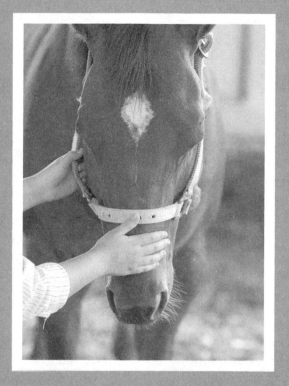

He was a different kind of horse from the get-go. We met on one of those sweaty August afternoons that hang motionless at the top of the thermometer. His nose and whiskers were all I could see of him over the half-door of the back stall. His curious snuffling stirred up lazy dust motes in the heavy air. The yearling's incessant huffing and the sound of his hooves puttering in the wood shavings were a welcome sign of life and sufficient to move me out of my heat-induced stupor.

The Morgan foal was here on consignment from a nearby breeder. Close up, he was even cuter than his prehensile nose and long, black whiskers had suggested. Big bug-eyes looked me over as I leaned my elbows on the top of the door. He sniffed me and used that upper lip to check my T-shirt, run an identity check on me, and assess the possibility that food or escape might be in the offing. He waited to see what I was planning before continuing his inspection of his new home.

I petted his thick forelock, scratched his chin, and went back to work. The farm manager had lured me to the barn on a steamy day when I didn't have any lessons scheduled, and she was still chuckling over it. She'd known my curiosity would get the better of me. On the phone she'd said, "You've gotta get over here quick! There's a huge rat in the back stall, and you *have* to see it!" She got me. The little guy's nose and whiskers poking over that door certainly did look like they belonged to the world's biggest rodent. His registered name was elegant, but that day he acquired the one that would stick with him for life: he became "the Rat."

My daughter was twelve and already had a generic gelding, but she longed for the thrill of breaking and training a horse on her own. So this was how we wound up at lunch with her grandfather, who had a ready checkbook and a sappy adoration for his only granddaughter. By the end of the meal, she had a check in her hand, and I felt a huge headache coming on. I clucked disapprovingly, but the conspirators had worked a deal that I couldn't argue with. He'd buy the colt and pay a year's board, and she'd do the scut work of getting the yearling ready to show, with an eye toward selling him for a profit in a year or two.

As will happen, "a year or two" stretched a bit. There were tears and bruises on all sides, but the yearling Morgan with the intelligent expression and near-human sense of humor got trained in spite of us all. He was far smarter than we were. Within months he'd figured out how to stand in places from which removing him would be challenging—if not dangerous. He used this talent to keep his busy brain occupied while avoiding onerous labor. Not that he found all work objectionable, but his quick mind was easily bored. Left to his own devices, he found things to do. More often than not, the ringing phone meant another dash to the barn to watch in awe as he demonstrated his newest achievement.

He spent days working his way into and out of abandoned coils of barbed wire in the pasture. That prehensile upper lip proved helpful in removing all the bolts from the gutter on the shed row eaves. His powers of observation were keen, so it was no surprise that he figured out how to carefully dismantle a saddle and bury the parts in the footing of the indoor arena. A discarded longe whip was perfect for driving the other horses in circles. His head bobbed wildly to make the popper fly up and down until his pasture mates were sweaty and tired. Like a nightclub comic, he played to his audience.

The Rat moved in and took over our world. Not only was he the funniest horse in the herd, he was also the best ride. Anyone old enough (or young enough) to sit upright could ride the Rat. His patience was legendary, his gait smooth as silk. Cocky teenaged boys rode him bareback before they had ever set butt in a saddle. Frightened toddlers regained their composure when he refused to move a muscle until they gave him the go-ahead. He followed me around the arena carrying riders who had no clue what to do with the reins. My daughter jumped him bareback over anything in her path. He matured to a whopping 14.3 hands, but in his mind he was as big or as small as we needed him to be.

The years stretched on some more, and the Rat ran the barn with a hearty political finesse. Never one to get mired in personal issues, he played with the horses who would play with him and ignored the ones who wouldn't. He grazed next to all of them equally. When the one-eyed horse came to board with us, Rat took over as social director. He seemed personally concerned about the new guy's fearfulness and lack of social élan. The Rat followed him like a dog for weeks, discussing, one might assume, how a new horse might best work himself into the herd. Where talk failed, action finally succeeded. In one unmistakable gesture, Rat cornered the new horse, and, when the dust settled, licked him from the top of his head to his hooves, from front to back, and around again. Then, his job done to his satisfaction, he trotted off, leaving the new horse to recover in private.

Knowledgeable horsemen will tell you that a child and a young horse are a bad mix. "Green horse, green rider," they'll *tsk tsk!*, shaking their heads. I agree completely, with one exception. My daughter and her Morgan were perfect together. Once the initial craziness of learning while she was teaching had passed, they bonded like siblings. It was *My Friend Flicka* come to life. They bickered endlessly. "Stop touching me! I *told* you to stop *touching me!*" I'd peek down the aisle and see Rat in the ties using that nose to just barely touch his girl on her shoulder or the back of her head, just enough to be irritating, not enough to warrant punishment. He'd move his hind end away just as she hoisted the saddle, and his big eyes would sparkle merrily when she howled in frustration. Every now and then she'd whack him with her hand when he was apparently standing perfectly still. "*He* knows what he's doing wrong, even if I don't!"

This would have been an idyllic span of years had life not continually touched us with chaos. The horses had been a security blanket I'd dragged from out of my past during my divorce. I had been off horses for years, but the need to feel whole and sane during the upheaval was strong, and I filled my world with their familiar smell and sound and feel. They kept my young daughter happy and busy and kept me feeling like I still had some connection to the person I thought I was.

But there was more going on. With little warning, my daughter began to come apart. An undiagnosed syndrome following an orthodontic error laced her body with pain. Errors in treatment and endless suffering were to become her permanent lot in life. I lived every parent's nightmare as her heartrending periods of agony were punctuated by sudden disastrous turns.

She muddled through. After each episode, her first thought was to get to the barn. Her older gelding, Grady, was still her favorite, but he was a tad spunky for someone as fragile as she sometimes was. The Rat, however, was a rock. No matter how bad things were, no matter how sick she felt from trials of new medications, or how much pain a new procedure caused, if she could drag herself onto his broad back, the Rat would take care of her. Slowly and carefully, he walked where she aimed him, and when she felt better he'd slip into a floating trot. In no time, she would be galloping over jumps, smiling and bright-eyed. During the bad times, I rarely heard, "Now *cut that out!*" coming from the barn. Rat knew when he could push and when he needed to just be.

Luck and strength were with her as she finished high school and made the huge leap of courage that took her away to college. The Rat stayed behind. At first she made weekly pilgrimages home, the barn always her first stop. As time went by, she found she didn't need the security quite as badly, and she stayed away for longer periods.

During those times, Rat turned his attention to me, and one bitter winter day, I was privileged to receive just a small taste of what my daughter had accepted from him for years. It was my second winter on the farm. The first year had been difficult enough. I'd run out of money long before I could install plumbing and lighting in the barn. I had fallen from the loft ladder and hurt my back, skated on the frozen hayfield and injured my knee, and developed knuckles the size of jawbreakers. The second winter brought pneumonia. There's nothing like mucking stalls in ten-degree weather with a burning fever and clogged lungs. This was a one-woman show with no intermission.

The Rat and I made contact at the height of my illness. It was early—just after dawn—and I sat huddled in the tack room, trying not to die while the horses ate breakfast. Silence heralded empty buckets, and I opened the stalls to let the animals into the pasture. It wasn't like Rat to linger, but that day he did. He was still near the gate when I dragged my body outside to close it. That done, I couldn't move another step. Crossing my arms over the top fence board, I rested my forehead and waited for the world to stop dimming out on me. My knees threatened to buckle as my fever soared. I sensed Rat near my elbow, but I couldn't do anything about it. Out of the corner of my misted eyes I saw him dip that squirmy lip into the snow. Ever so gently, the Rat dusted the back of my neck with his nose. Again into the snow his nose went, and again he brushed my neck gently. I felt the heat melting the snow on contact, the cool dampness bringing me around just enough. I couldn't talk—no breathing, no talking—but I patted the horse on the head, thanked him mentally, and staggered back to the house. Glancing behind me, I saw Rat still standing at the gate. He stayed there, his huge eyes following my progress, until I closed the door behind me. Then he finished his trip to the pasture to stand with his buddies. I understood that morning what it was that had sustained my daughter through the worst of the worst. Corny as it sounds, an overwhelming feeling of confidence and peace came from that horse in waves.

Time passed. My young daughter became a woman and, finally, a bride. When the day came for her to take her belongings and set up her own household some hundred miles away, I felt a moment of panic. I wanted to hold onto her, but also, jealously, I wanted to hide the Rat so she couldn't take him along. It was a moment of insanity soon subdued by rational thought. She needed him. She had a long road ahead filled with pain and illness and uncertainty. I loved them both, but I loved her more. Without Rat, she wouldn't make it, of that I was certain. I watched dry-eyed as she loaded Rat into the trailer with her

Thoroughbred mare and left me with a cloud of dust and some big empty spaces.

It's been a while now. There is still something missing from the farm, but some things just don't bear replacing. I sleep a little better knowing that, in the worst of times, my baby will be safe on the Rat's broad back and in the shelter of his spirit. He's a big little horse with stories yet to tell, and I'm honored to have crossed his trail.

—Joanne M. Friedman

Chanson de Roland

I was first introduced to Roland when I started taking polo lessons with Lester Crossman. Then in his sixties, Les had been teaching polo to novices for decades. He had played for one of the country's first polo clubs, the Myopia Polo Club in Massachusetts, through forty-five of its ninety-five years. He was still playing when I met him.

A gruff, no-nonsense old-timer, Les sized up people and horses at a glance and then assigned them to each other. He assigned me to Roland. The appendix Thoroughbred had come from out West through a dealer who knew what Les liked in a polo pony. Not only did Roland have the perfect build for polo, he was so even tempered and good natured that Les used him to teach his students as well as for competitive play. Roland competed at Palm Beach, throughout the Northeast, and in the finals of many prestigious national tournaments. When I had the good fortune to meet this remarkable horse, Roland had already retired back to Lester's farm in Danvers, Massachusetts.

At our first encounter, he looked at me from his stall and gave a combination snort and nicker. He seemed to say, *Oh no, not another new one*, but at the same time, *Maybe you would like to give me a carrot to win my favor?* He was not at all head shy, sticking his face out to be rubbed, even pushing you with it if he believed you had something in your hand. But his eyes smiled as he did it; if he knocked you over, you would know he really didn't mean it.

I don't know if I ever really learned to play polo. My rating never exceeded one goal—out of a possible ten. But Roland certainly knew the game: he could anticipate the direction of play and begin to turn just from hearing the sound of the ball being struck. No matter whether we were in an indoor arena or on an outdoor field, he always got me to the ball. He also knew when someone needed riding off the line of the ball and how to do it. Bigger horses didn't faze him. Roland would get lower, push up with his shoulder, and lift the other horse off his stride. Roland and I played five seasons together.

Roland didn't excel just at polo: he was bombproof. I could rely on him as a mount for visitors, whether the children of friends or visiting television celebrities like Alex Cord and Steve Bond, who came to play charity polo for the March of Dimes. He always took care of his rider first, whether on trail rides, beach rides, or fox hunts.

Roland was smart, too. His rare talent for opening gates and stalls allowed him to come up to the kitchen to see what we were having for breakfast. Sometimes he would let my whole string out, so his stall mates could trot down the driveway and visit the neighbors. Once he led them to the village center where the local constabulary chased them before the horses stopped to graze. While his "gang" would scurry about if approached, Roland knew when the jig was up and stood patiently for the halter. He was the only one I had to catch, because the whole delinquent crew would follow him back to their stalls. It was pretty clear who the alpha gelding was.

Roland's last career, in an entirely new discipline, began when he was about twenty-one years old. He became a mount at Windrush Farm Therapeutic Equitation, one of the oldest therapeutic riding centers in the United States. Roland was soon a stalwart in the program, gently supporting disabled children in the saddle, and providing a reliable mount for many disabled riders at the Massachusetts Equestrian Special Olympics and at regional shows affiliated with the North American Riding for the Handicapped Association. He also schooled new riders and became the most popular horse at Windrush's summer camp for able-bodied children.

As Roland enjoyed his new job, I rode other horses. In October 1994, as I was riding with the Myopia Hunt Club, my mount tripped. I was thrown and suffered a T6-7 spinal cord injury. While I couldn't move from the chest down, I still had the use of my arms. After a long recovery, I received a scholarship from Windrush to participate in therapeutic equitation to complement my physical therapy and rehabilitation.

I began my program on a very quiet horse, but my goal—and one of the major reasons I even tried to ride—was to ride Roland once more. That goal helped me face the glaring contrasts between my life before and after the accident and the reality of the riding skills I had lost. I hadn't been a great rider even before the accident, but I had played polo competitively, ridden to hounds well enough to earn my colors and whip-in, and competed at the novice level in combined training.

Roland knew my voice and nickered a greeting whenever I came for a lesson. He was as patient teaching me to ride again as he was when he first taught me to play polo. Many times when I leaned out too far, he would scoot under me to keep me from falling. Roland sensed my vulnerability and kept me safe. Some people joked that he didn't notice a difference, since I wasn't noted for using my legs very well before the accident. But Roland noticed. As I said, he was smart. Eventually, after many lessons, Roland and I could perform demonstration rides, two at the Groton House Farms Horse Trials where I'd competed as an able-bodied rider.

In winter 2000, eight years after he started at Windrush, Roland seemed listless and uncomfortable. We all agreed that he should retire and I gladly brought him home, where we rode together one last time on the trails surrounding my house.

As a final cap to his two careers, I nominated Roland for the Cosequin Exemplary Service Award. He had provided service to riders of various ages and abilities, riding and competing in more than one discipline. He embodied the giving spirit of a remarkable and noble species with whom we humans have the privilege of sharing our planet. I submitted his story, hoping to give Roland the recognition he deserved. For his part, Roland was just happy to know I had nominated him and nickered, as usual, for the expected pat on the nose and carrot. The selection committee agreed with me and chose Roland out of hundreds of nominees to be named the 2001 Exemplary Equine Service Horse of the Year. I accepted the award on Roland's behalf, donating the proceeds to Windrush. Roland was not there.

A few months before the award ceremony, Roland had spent a weekend standing in the corner of the paddock closest to the house. He seemed to support himself on the post-and-rail fencing. I feared the worst, but felt I needed to be brave, so I rolled my wheelchair across the lawn to take him some carrots. He nickered, as always, and then rested his head gently in my lap, letting me support its weight in a way he had never done before. He sighed, as if to bid me farewell.

When I was away from home the next week, Roland fell where he had been standing. He was buried overlooking the countryside he loved and knew so well, on a hill where he had many times watched riders and hounds race past. His spirit now runs with them. One day, if I am fortunate, I will find his kind and generous soul one last time. I will saddle him, he will wonder why it is taking me so long, and we will ride together again.

Roland was the name of Charlemagne's most famous companion, a loyal, courageous, and perfect knight who defended his fallen comrades and sacrificed himself in service to his king. I can't help but notice the similarities. My Roland gave of himself to all his riders, young or old, disabled or able-bodied, in competition or for pleasure. He could not heal my broken back, but he certainly did much to heal my soul and take away the despair and loneliness I often felt looking at life from the vantage point of a wheelchair. When I was on his back and in his care, only then did I move as I remembered. Only then did I really look the world in the eye. Such is the power of horses to heal man. Such was Roland's power to heal me.

—Paul A. Spiers, Ph.D.

Kelly Comes Through

I'm ba-ack! taunted the jinx.
Ellis thought borrowing Kinley Gold had exorcised
it, but when the big bay refused a critical jump
during her Pony Club rating, she realized her hex
had only pretended to leave. The examiner told

her she could not complete the test, and the seventeen-year-old exited the arena in humiliation.

"Whatever I do, it doesn't work," Ellis whispered hoarsely into Kinley's mane. "It's just no use!"

This was the second time she'd ridden someone else's mount in a Pony Club test. Her own horse, Storm, pulled a suspensory ligament just before the previous test. Because the vet sanctioned Storm's return to work too early, the gelding immediately renewed the injury, dooming Ellis's chances of passing this next rating.

The persistent jinx seemed banished when I lent her my eventer, Kinley Gold. The talented bay was not in full work, and he takes being ignored personally. Here was a perfect opportunity for him to feel loved and useful again and for Ellis to get back in the saddle.

There were only three weeks before the August test, so the teenager began training immediately. She was not going to waste this chance, so she came to ride at my yard every evening after interning at the local vet's, as well as plowing through a heavy reading schedule for school.

The Irish Draught half of Kinley loathes dressage and exacts tremendous effort from his rider. But Ellis persevered, Kinley's grass paunch receded, and the pair soon developed a rapport.

Kinley's Thoroughbred genes made the stadium and cross-country exercises fun. Ellis had only to point the horse at a fence and he would sail over it, so her instructor added higher obstacles to boost her confidence. All was going brilliantly.

On the day before the rating, Ellis arrived to clean the tack. Her mom, Jill, helped beautify an amazed and gratified Kinley, who, looking superb, eyed me accusingly, *You're never this thorough!*

We decided Kinley should stay inside overnight and conserve his energy. At 5 P.M. I put him out in the small paddock for a few hours with his buddy, Double Clover, before bringing them back in for the night. Kinley hates horseflies, and when one landed on the middle of his rump—where his tail couldn't reach—he went beserk, galloping and bucking around the limited space to escape it. Worried he would hurt himself, I returned both geldings to their fan-cooled stalls.

Despite Double Clover's company, Kinley found the change in his routine stressful, so I decided that his staying out all night would be less detrimental than colicking from tension indoors. There were now no flies, and he grazed happily with the other horses.

By six o'clock the next morning, Ellis and her mom were polishing my horse again, and a glistening Kinley loaded into the trailer for the short trip to the local hunt club.

Ellis longed for the riding to begin as she endured the first part of the Pony Club test: tack inspection followed by leg bandaging. Thirty minutes later, she and Heather, the other girl being examined, were warming up their mounts in the sand arena. At 16.2 hands high, Kinley looked huge compared to Heather's diminutive pony, Domingo. All of us—parents and assorted well-wishers—relaxed on canvas chairs to watch this fun phase.

It started out fun, but then Kinley wouldn't give Ellis her canter lead to the right. As they trotted around for another try, I thought, "Is he moving short behind?" When Ellis got the correct canter, I decided I had been seeing things. Kinley popped through a grid and over the lower fences and a three-foot upright. Thank goodness, he was okay!

But Ellis's jinx was toying with her. She approached the three-foot oxer on a good stride with plenty of impulsion—and Kinley ducked out. Tiny Domingo cleared it with ease.

Ellis brought Kinley around for another try. A second refusal. She put him at it again, and once more he said *No*.

I saw the misery on her parents' faces and felt terrible. What was wrong? In spite of Storm's multiple injuries, this was supposed to be Ellis's big day, and now her hex was striking again. As it happened, Kinley had hurt himself running from that fly. It would turn out to be a minor sprain, but that didn't help Ellis now. We all felt sorry for the dejected teenager as she was told to leave the ring.

Seeing her eviction I relived my own past snubs by the horse world—that club I desperately wanted to join as a teenager, which continually rejected me because they said my mount and I weren't good enough. Now my own horse was inflicting the same pain on someone else! I felt like a traitor who had raised Ellis's hopes only to dash them at the crucial moment.

"What did the examiner say?" I asked, as she fiddled miserably with Kinley's mane.

"He's lame. I can't continue."

She'd put so much time and effort into him. Riding without stirrups to strengthen her legs and combat his sluggishness; spending all those hours cleaning him and his tack. It was grossly unfair that all had gone wrong. There had to be a way to solve this. I asked Ellis to let me think a moment, and she nodded, tears welling in her eyes. My mind churned furiously, assessing the other horses back home. Could any of them take Ellis through her rating? The five-year-old was too inexperienced, and Double Clover's jumping was unpredictable. My twenty-five-year-old mare, Kelly, was a faint possibility, but she was so unlike Kinley! He was tall and solid, whereas she was a slight Thoroughbred, barely 15.3 hands high. They couldn't be more different.

Then I remembered chatting with Ellis about Storm. She'd described her horse as a small, forward-going chestnut—and that defined my mare, too. It just might work. Kelly had been off for a year and a half with a tendon sheath injury. The vet had told me she'd never jump again, but I had refused to accept his diagnosis. Thanks to homeopathic treatments, rest, and TLC, she had recovered. Still, it was a long shot.

"How would you feel about trying Kelly?" I asked. My voice sounded artificially upbeat. Ellis looked at me in shock, which she struggled to overcome. "I don't know—I've never ridden her," she managed to say.

"But you've seen me ride her, and you've invested so much in this test. It's a real pity to give up now."

"We-ell . . . " The slim teenager thought about it. "Does she jump?"

"She *loves* jumping! And she's much more like your horse than Kinley. I think you'd feel very comfortable on her."

Ellis accepted this argument before her face clouded over again. "But she's so old. Supposing I hurt her?"

"You won't. She's in regular training, plus I jumped her only yesterday. She's fit and ready to go."

I'd brought the mare back into work when Ellis borrowed Kinley, not because I'd planned any shows for her, but because her son, Cruz Bay, was recovering from proud flesh removal. Now I understood why it "so happened" that Kelly had jumped three-foot fences—the height Ellis needed—only the day before. I suddenly realized a higher power was at work here, and I knew Ellis could do it. I turned to her mom. I wanted her approval before her daughter took this leap into the unknown.

"Jill, would you be okay with that?"

"If Ellis is," came her immediate answer.

Her supportive attitude was a relief, but then I read the teenager's thoughts. Storm was hurt, now Kinley was hurt—what was to stop a third disaster?

I looked at her squarely. "Ellis, you have nothing to lose, and everything to gain. It's asking real guts from you to do this, but Kelly's a good horse—she'll take you around."

The dispirited rider took a deep breath and said, "Okay!" Ellis was ready to fight her jinx.

The idea was cleared with the patient Pony Club examiner, and I trailered the short distance to my house to collect Kelly. I hoped no one would check her ancient though serviceable tack, or scrutinize my emergency grooming.

Because I was in a hurry, Kelly refused to load. Since there was no time to argue with her, I would have to ride her to the club. At least the mare would be warmed up. I've never tacked a horse up so fast in my life.

The minutes were ticking by so I chose the quickest route. Thanks to the previous day's rain and the efforts of that beastly jinx, Kelly twice lost her hind end sliding down an unavoidable mud bank. "Now she's going to be lame as well!" I wailed inwardly. But I said a quick prayer to her equine guardian angel and kept going.

If Ellis regretted her courageous decision by the time we came into view, she didn't show it. But she asked a smart question as she mounted: "Has anyone ever ridden her besides you?"

I truthfully replied, "Yes," without adding that it had been a few years ago.

Her parents and I held our breath as the girl rode back into the arena on my feisty mare. Ellis is a very quiet rider, which is exactly what Kelly likes. The warm-up went smoothly, and this time there were no problems with canter strike offs. The chestnut was too quick through the jump grid, so the examiner removed Ellis's spurs, which she'd needed with Kinley, but were now serious overkill. Riding confidently, Ellis cleared all the fences, including Kinley's bugbear oxer. She left the ring beaming from ear to ear. Relieved, her mother, father, and I were also smiling as we walked with her to the cross-country course.

But Ellis caught the mare unawares at the first log, and she stopped.

Ha!, cried the jinx.

"No!" I countered and telepathically messaged Ellis, "Wake her up!" The examiner was more helpful and gave an instruction verbally. Over they popped. The mare happily jumped up and down a bank, cleared another log, and cantered with Ellis to the final fence, an intimidating square oxer. But by now Ellis was completely comfortable with her new mount, and they cleared it in grand style. When Heather's diminutive pony leaped over it too, we all cheered and began breathing again.

Ellis dismounted and rushed over to me. "I *have* to give you a big hug!" the normally reserved girl cried. She added, "Jumping Kelly was like coming home to my own horse." I squeezed her in admiration. "I would never have had the courage to do what you've just done. Congratulations!"

Ellis did much more than pass her rating that day. With Kelly's help, she exhibited the tremendous horsemanship she'd been capable of all along. By riding a strange horse, she also inadvertently passed a section of her next Pony Club rating. And she found the courage to chase away her jinx for good.

Back in her stall, I hugged Kelly for the umpteenth time and gave her one more treat. "You're a superstar, you broke Ellis's hex!" The old mare yawned, *Yeah, yeah, whatever.* This flattery business was getting old. She munched on her hay, pointedly ignoring me, before those enormous brown eyes softened toward me again with a twinkle.

I guess I am a bit special, aren't I?

—Hilary C. T. Walker

Belle

Belle was a dangerous horse and seemed to be a lost cause. Those who knew her were concerned that she would someday seriously hurt or even kill someone. For me, she was the challenge I needed to take my mind off a great loss.

I was eighteen weeks pregnant and extremely excited, anticipating the wonderful sound of my growing baby's heartbeat. At an ultrasound appointment two weeks later, I was informed that my little girl had died. The news devastated me and sent me into a depression that no one could pull me out of. I didn't want to do anything, not even work or ride. My husband, Brad, and I tried again a couple months later, but I lost that pregnancy at six weeks. Having a family was looking pretty hopeless. That thought sent me deeper into depression, and there wasn't much that anyone could say or do to help.

As a horse trainer who specializes in colts and problem horses, you would think that my work alone would have taken my mind off my loss, but it didn't. Soon after I lost the second pregnancy, I spotted a beautiful palomino mare in my neighbor's pasture. Kathie had bought Belle a few months before with plans to turn her into a professional barrel racing horse. Belle had a different plan. She bronced (not bucked, *bronced*) Kathie off and hurt her badly, and she did the same to anyone else who tried to ride her. The only solution was to forget barrel racing and let her be a bucking horse at rodeos.

Kathie took Belle to two different stock contractors hoping they would buy her, or that Belle would hate it so much she would stop bucking. No such luck! In fact, she was turning into a pretty good bareback bronc. But the contractors didn't want to pay Kathie's asking price, so she brought Belle back home, and that's when I saw her in the pasture. I suggested to Kathie that she let me try the horse and see if I could figure out what was wrong with her.

"No way!" she said. "I don't want you or anyone else to get hurt on her."

Since trying her was out of the question, I decided to buy her, using the money I'd saved for the baby. Kathie wasn't too thrilled with that idea, either, but finally she agreed—with one small requirement. She said I could buy Belle if I could ride her for one week without her bucking. One week! The idea seemed impossible. Belle just came from a string of bucking horses. She had ringworm and flank marks and she would come unglued if you even touched her side with a finger. But I had one week and the challenge was on.

That week consisted of a crash course in round penning, ground driving, and getting on. I worked with Belle a couple times a day. At the end of the week I rode her for Kathie and told her that I *did* ride Belle, and she didn't buck. The horse had flipped over, but flipping over wasn't part of the deal, so I didn't mention it. Was she broke? No way. But she was mine, and she had done what I had hoped she would do: she had taken my mind off my loss. When I worked with Belle, I had no time to think of anything but what I was doing. I knew I could make something of her, but I wasn't sure exactly what that "something" would be.

A month after purchasing Belle, my husband and I decided to move from Colorado to Wyoming. Just at that time, I found out I was pregnant again. I willed myself not to get too excited and hopeful this time. I would just keep my mind on Belle, and I rode her every day without fail.

I decided to try to turn Belle into a barrel racing horse, since that was what Kathie had originally planned for her. There was just one problem: I wasn't a barrel racer. When I was seven I had dreamed of one day being a professional barrel racer like the pretty ones I saw at the rodeos. The only barrel-racing experience I could remember was when my horse ran home with me after rounding the first barrel in the 4-H county fair when I was ten. My experience was in showing American Saddlebreds, and I had ventured into a few other disciplines, such as reining and dressage.

"What the heck," I thought. "Why not try it now?" I bought some books and started to teach myself—and my horse—how to barrel race the right way. As I got bigger throughout my pregnancy, I learned that I had to keep Belle moving slowly. Running a pattern was out of the question, so we did a lot of slow work and trotted for miles and miles. The result was that Belle got in fabulous shape. It amazed me to see Belle grow calmer as I grew bigger. I was convinced that she knew I was pregnant and didn't want to hurt my baby or me.

I rode Belle until two weeks before I had Chance, our beautiful baby boy. I returned to riding in the week after delivery; I knew I couldn't give Belle too much time off. The first day I got back on her, she bucked and went over sideways. I let her into the round pen to buck, but quickly learned that was the wrong thing to do with this horse. With Belle, everything had to be controlled.

After Chance was born I could finally take Belle out in the open and let her run as fast and as far as she wanted. I wanted to see if my horse had any speed to her. I was happy to learn that she was, in a word, *fast*. She was not only fast, but she was in such good shape from all the trotting that she had stamina as well. So off to the barrels we went.

Brad and I then decided to move back to Colorado to be closer to family. I boarded my horses up the hill from Kathie's place. Only ten acres separated me from her arena. On days we practiced, I packed up the stroller with diapers and bottles, blankets and burp rags and walked Chance down the hill with Belle following close behind.

Kathie gave me pointers and encouraged me to enter some 4D barrel races. The 4Ds are good for someone like me, because there are four divisions to place in. The fastest time of the day sets division one. Division two is half a second slower, division three is one second slower, and division four is two seconds slower. I was three seconds behind the fastest time of the day, but I still won a check. That year I won quite a few checks, and by the following year I was setting the time of the day. People were amazed—*I* was amazed—and Kathie was thrilled. I won the Rookie of the Year Award and the Equine Achievement Award. I did so well my first year that I decided to get my permit with the Women's Professional Rodeo Association and try the pro rodeo circuit. With a couple lessons from World Champion Kristie Peterson, I started down that road and did extremely well. I was always within the top times and I won quite a few checks. Maybe I could be that professional barrel racer that I dreamed about when I was seven. It was a starter year for Belle and me. We weren't the best, but at least we now had an idea of what to do. We were ready and excited for the year to come. All we had to do was get through the Colorado winter.

The holidays were not very merry. A few days before Christmas, Belle came up from the pasture with an extremely lame left hind leg. The vet thought she might have an abscess, since she didn't show signs of anything else. I soaked the foot, but when it didn't get any better I took her back to the vet for x-rays. On Christmas Eve, I learned that Belle had shattered a bone in her leg. There was nothing to do but stretch it, cast it, and wait for the bone to fuse together. Her barrel racing days were over. Most people would have put her down, but I couldn't. She had saved my life. Without even knowing it, Belle put the life that I had lost back into me. She had given me hope and pulled me out of a depression when no one else could. She was my savior. I had to help Belle. By this time, I was pregnant with my second son, Blake. But this time it was my horse I worried about.

The surgeon suggested that Belle be sent to a barn where veterinary students and interns could watch over her. My vet quickly intervened and said it was a bad idea. He told the surgeon that Belle would never recover fully anywhere but home, and that I was the only one who could give her the drive to heal. My outlook for her had to change, so I began to make plans to breed her after her recovery.

Belle spent four months in a cast and a year in a stall. She had lost a few hundred pounds during her surgeries. It felt like forever, but I finally got to breed her a year and a half later.

On Mother's Day, her first foal was born—a filly! All I could do was cry. I shed tears of joy and tears of remembering all that Belle and I had been through. She had helped me through a time when I needed something special and inspirational. I had helped her through a time when she needed to lean on me. And, coming full circle, we both got our little girl.

—Tami Bova

Mitchell's Journey

When I am riding a horse
I can imagine all my dreams are sweet.
—from "Imagine a Horse"
by Mitchell Yeoh

I glanced at my son, Mitchell, now
nine, pacing the floor in circles. This
was his usual dance, along with the
hand-flapping tick and a high-pitched

squeal of delight. This was a normal occurrence in our house, especially when he was excited about something.

Mitchell has Asperger's syndrome, a high-functioning form of autism. He was diagnosed in kindergarten. I will never forget the day when the school called us in for a meeting, and we sat there, drowning in papers. Numb was all I felt as they explained autism, as if my husband and I had been living on another planet and had to have medical jargon defined for us. I sat there staring at the papers. "Now what? What else could be wrong with our beautiful boy?" I thought, but didn't say.

Mitchell had already been through enough physical pain to last him a lifetime. Before he was born he was diagnosed with a rare and incurable condition called autosomal recessive polycystic kidney disease. We had lost a daughter to the same illness; she'd lived only sixteen hours. My husband and I traveled from institution to institution, desperate to save the son we could see growing in the ultrasound images, but we were offered no hope. One doctor said, "Just expect what happened to your daughter to happen to your son." Finally, we found a high-risk obstetrician willing to help us.

Mitchell was born on a cold, snowy February day. His abdomen was so enlarged that he looked as if he were nine months pregnant. I could see his swollen kidneys through his skin. Every minute counted. We transported him—just four weeks old and barely alive—to California on a private plane, stealing away like thieves in the night. There, it would be a transplant surgeon's job to save him. Both kidneys were removed and a dialysis catheter inserted in their place. Not only did I need to learn how to care for a newborn with diaper changes and late-night feedings, but I also had to learn how to give him shots, insert tubes in his nose, draw medicine, and work a dialysis machine to keep him alive. Later, I was able to donate a kidney, and Mitchell eventually had a transplant.

We longed for Mitchell to have a "normal" childhood, but it was impossible. How could one travel through hell and back and be normal? My husband and I were denied that carefree wonder of watching a child grow and develop that most new parents enjoyed. Instead, our minds raced with thoughts: "What if he falls and ruptures his spleen? Will he talk and walk?" Although the transplant was successful, and Mitchell was thriving, we knew that it wasn't a permanent cure and that his follow-up care would be extensive. No one else knew the depth of our anguish or fully understood the lengths we had traveled to get Mitchell to where he is now. We celebrate every day of his life and try hard to make it normal amid worries about germs from other kids or innumerable doctor's appointments.

Despite all his physical challenges, Mitchell's mind grew by leaps and bounds. Early on, he learned multiplication and division, the alphabet in sixteen languages, and writing in print and script. He drew like Picasso, studied Shakespeare's plays, and could identify musical composers as well as their works. Soon Mitchell was fluent in four languages, without formal training. We sought opinions from professionals about his gift. But, as Mitchell said so brilliantly, "My blessing is a curse, Mommy," paraphrasing Shakespeare's *Twelfth Night*. The child psychologist was baffled. He thought Mitchell might have autism, but with so many savant qualities, it was hard to say. When Mitchell reached kindergarten, our fears were confirmed. The delays we thought were merely physical were distracting us from the real issue.

Asperger's was yet another blow. Another challenge. Another heartbreak.

Mitchell interrupted his dance long enough to try to get my attention, "Mommy, hurry or we are going to be late! Horses! Horses! We're going to the farm!" I stopped brooding long enough to realize that my son, whose body was riddled with scars, who could hardly walk a straight line without bumping into something, was going to ride a horse!

We arrived very early for his first ride. I knew from long experience that once Mitchell was out of the car, there would be no chance of reeling him back in. Mitchell counted the seconds until his ride, first in German, then in Russian, Chinese, and so on. Finally, it was time to meet everyone. Mitchell flung open the door like a horse out of the starting gate. I thought he might explode with excitement. He ran straight to the beautiful, faded red barn. A little corgi came up to greet us. The setting was like a picture postcard, and so different from the busy street we lived on. Mitchell made his way through the barn, saying "Hello" and introducing himself, all the while skipping and squealing with delight. I commented to Lois, the physical therapist, that I had never seen him so excited. I wanted to explain how serious and studious he usually was. No one could know how really happy this outing made him.

Finally, Lois calmed Mitchell down and explained the rules. I could tell he was taking it in, despite his inability to stand still or look her in the eye. As he put on his helmet, I realized I had forgotten my camera. With Mitchell's liver failing rapidly, we never knew when he would need more surgery. "What if he never got to ride again?" If I'd brought the camera, he could have looked at his picture in the hospital and remembered this day.

I was still scolding myself as my son climbed the mounting block and waited for Annie, a gentle and beautiful sandy-colored appaloosa. "She has sweet eyes," I thought. As Annie approached the block, I could tell Mitchell was nervous, so I knew how badly he wanted this ride. Annie seemed to know how much he wanted and needed her, too, and stood very still as he climbed on her back. My soul was soaring as I watched Mitchell sit tall in the saddle. No one seeing him sit so proudly on that majestic creature could perceive the hell he had been through. After his ride, Mitchell fed Annie a carrot and we started home.

My son rarely shares his feelings unless a therapist pulls them out of him. But Mitchell couldn't stop talking about Annie. "Mommy, it makes me want to imagine. She makes me so happy!" I had to stop the car to really pay attention to what he was saying.

"Why does Annie make you so happy?" Who, what, and why questions are very hard for him to answer, but he responded without hesitation.

"Annie makes me happy because I can feel proud that I can ride her, and I am just a small person."

I turned and smiled, trying to choke back the tears. "You should feel proud. You were very brave to ride such a big horse." He grinned from ear to ear, then let out a squeal, and a "Yes, ma'am!"

Soon after we arrived home, Mitchell got out his paints and paper and painted a picture of Annie eating a carrot. When he finished, he stroked the painting sweetly and sighed, "I love you, Annie." I'd have given anything to be Annie at that moment. People with Asperger's usually show very little emotion, so this was no small occurrence.

Mitchell has come a long way since his first ride on Annie. Riding has opened up a whole new world for him. Now he gives more eye contact, converses with others, and asks questions without prompting—all things the therapists at school have been trying to get him to do for years. He writes prolifically about horses in his school journal. Riding has done all this for him in a few weeks. Now he rides a horse named Classy. Their bond is beyond amazing. Long ago I heard that animals were good for autistic kids. We had tried to interest him in many different animals at home, but Mitchell would have nothing to do with any of them. The horse was pure magic.

I don't know what spell the horses cast over Mitchell. Part of his response may be that he's never had control over his illness. Perhaps when he's riding his mind is cleared of the clutter of constant thinking. Perhaps, as he wrote in one of his poems, the horses allow him to have "wonderful and magical dreams." Whatever it is, it's pure and simple and beyond human comprehension.

And horses have helped me, too. I feel as though I've been given a break from worrying about my son's medical woes. When I look at Mitchell sitting tall in the saddle, his illnesses seem to vanish. He is a beautiful boy on a beautiful animal.

—Lezah Yeoh

Finding My Prince Charming

There I sat on the dock overlooking Juanita Bay. I'd just turned fifty, I had never been married, I had been diagnosed an incomplete quadriplegic ten years earlier, and my disability had recently ended my professional career. As the tears streamed down my face, my heart cried out, "What did I do to deserve such joy?"

At a time when I'd all but given up any hope of falling in love, I had met my soul mate—a man with integrity, a man who shared my dreams and goals, a man who had fallen as hopelessly in love with my spirit as I had his. This story began when I unexpectedly found a place that would help heal my soul and prepare my heart for love. The year I had turned forty, I was struck with a condition that left me partially paralyzed and dependent on a motorized wheelchair. For several years, I looked for activities I could participate in, since the ones I used to enjoy were no longer available to me. For reasons I don't understand, therapeutic horseback riding appealed to me. I had never considered riding, even before my illness, but I contacted an organization that taught people with disabilities how to ride. When I made the call I thought I was only signing up for horseback riding lessons. I hadn't planned on a heart-altering metamorphosis.

Up to this time, the concept of love had totally eluded me. I would ask people, "What is love? How does it feel? Where do I find it?" Little did I know I would catch glimpses of it through my blossoming relationships with horses. Had it not been for my equine friends, I may not have recognized love when it walked around the corner of a stall in the shape of a man named Guy.

My lessons in love began one week after I registered for riding, when I found myself atop a large quarter horse named Scotchie. My instructor lovingly referred to Scotchie as a kind gentleman. All I saw was a huge, unpredictable animal. But over the next several months, I got to know him. He *was* a gentleman, carrying me carefully around the arena and over trails, always putting his rider's needs first. Gradually, he helped me learn how to maneuver and trust him. Scotchie was the perfect mount for a frightened novice like me. Unfortunately, my time with Scotchie was much too short. One beautiful sunny afternoon, he lay down under a tree and never got up again. Though he passed peacefully in his favorite place, I felt as if I'd lost my best friend.

Although I had loved Scotchie and missed him, I was surprised by the outpouring of love and deep sense of loss felt by our little community at the riding facility. At a service in the memorial garden, the staff and several students shared their fond and funny memories of Scotchie. I watched in amazement as grown men and women expressed their sorrow through poetry and tears. I had never seen such an open demonstration of love and loss, particularly for an animal. While I recognized the value of feeling the pain and mourning the loss, I envied those who could cry. I couldn't allow myself to feel that strongly about anything or anyone. Loss was too painful. I tried hard to overcome the barriers I had built up over the years against such feelings. It began to dawn on me that Scotchie not only had taught me about riding, but he had also begun to teach me how to accept love and loss in my life.

Around the time Scotchie died, Guy started volunteering at the barn, although I was oblivious to him. As a single woman, I thought my "husband radar" was always active, but Guy proved me wrong. When he approached me at a fundraising auction, it was apparent he knew who I was. "Do I know you?" was my inadequate response. My excuse was that he looked different in a tuxedo than he did in jeans, but I couldn't believe I had been so closed off that I hadn't noticed him before that moment.

From then on I did notice him, but my fear of relationships prevented me from taking any initiative. We would run into each other at infrequent events, and I would joke to my friends that this was the perfect way to get to know someone—in passing, twice a year. Granted, it meant we wouldn't be involved until we were eighty, but it fit perfectly within my comfort zone.

A retired Thoroughbred polo pony named JR inadvertently helped change all that. Any other rider would have found the antics of this friendly, well-trained, but slightly skittish horse laughable, but I wasn't any other rider. I was a nervous first-timer. JR's narrow back challenged my compromised balance, and his occasional sudden movements kept me off guard and anxious. One afternoon, he suddenly broke out in a sweat and collapsed. Although the instructor hauled me off before the colicky horse started to roll, the sense of helplessness and concern for the horse left me badly shaken. I continued to ride every week, but started to dread my lessons.

When a volunteer asked me why I still rode when riding scared me so much, I didn't have a very good answer. I came to realize that I enjoyed the horses and benefited from being around them. I was determined to overcome my fears. I have always believed that people without fears weren't courageous; it's the people who have fears and learn to conquer them who are the courageous ones. Without knowing it, JR was helping me conquer my fear of riding while building the courage to face other challenges in my life.

Guy and I continued to bump into each other. Although he didn't volunteer on the days I rode, I started to look for him around the barn and found the courage to seek him out. I knew I was interested in him, and he seemed to be interested in me. I looked forward to every chance meeting, but I still wasn't ready to go beyond the safety of the barn. What I needed were a few more lessons and a small twist of fate.

My instructor noticed my waning enthusiasm for riding JR, so she moved me to a quieter, wider horse named Murphy. He had deservedly won Horse of the Year awards several times at different levels, and soon he won my heart. While Murphy has the patience and kindness of a saint, he *is* a horse, with all the behavioral idiosyncrasies that entails. But, overall, this small draft horse loves working with disabled riders. He took this frightened rider and turned her into a competitor.

From the moment we were paired, Murphy took care of me, although I was slow to recognize it. His consistent gait reassured me before I even noticed it, and he was so in tune with the class that both my leader and I often thought the other one was directing him. Because of his quiet manner, Murphy was the first horse trained to use the new hoist in the mounting ramp. Patient and attentive, he stood quietly while I was lifted high above his head and lowered onto his back.

Over the next two years Murphy and I bonded. We were always happy to see one another and trusted each other implicitly. It was a relationship I never expected to have with anyone, let alone a horse, and one that I cherish and learn from every day. Murphy taught me about love and trust—two things I hadn't realized had been sorely lacking in my life.

While my relationships with the horses grew, fate decided to give Guy and me a push. During a three-day riding competition, I found myself spending quite a bit of time with him. We seemed to migrate toward each other whenever he had a break from his volunteer responsibilities, and we spent the time talking (and talking) and getting to know each other. As it turned out, we had a great deal in common, and I discovered that being in his company was a very comfortable place. Although I was increasingly open with him, my fear of intimacy still held me back whenever the conversation turned personal.

Lessons at the barn continued. Scotchie, JR, and Murphy had given me the courage and desire to advance my riding skills, but in order to really improve I needed a horse better trained for my physical needs, as well as one experienced in neck reining. When I heard that Scotchie's brother was available, I raced out to his stall to check him out. Sifter is a beautiful chestnut quarter horse—just like Scotchie, only with a bleach job: a flaxen mane and tail. More experienced riders call Sifter a "push-button pony"; I call him perfect. His easy manner and predictable responses immediately allowed me to ride independently, a goal of mine since I had started riding five years earlier. But what really sold me on Sifter was his even jog. His gait is so smooth that his back remains motionless as his legs move beneath him.

Sifter's even temperament and willingness have given me the confidence to compete. In 2005, I advanced from a walk-only equitation class to a walk-trot class. Although I tied for second in a class of three, I was proud of myself for pushing beyond my comfort zone in an effort to complete my best ride ever. With

Sifter's help, I now set my goals higher every year and experience the elation that comes from achieving those goals.

My newfound confidence was put to the test when fate threw Guy and me together one more time. We were the only two participants in a volunteer activity, and it was just the push we needed to begin spending time together outside of the barn. We seemed to take up right where we left off at the horse show, and before I realized it, we were dating. I had finally learned my lessons about love, courage, and trust. I opened up to the joy of feeling close to someone and the thrill of taking risks in matters of the heart. Guy and I were married six months later.

I have no idea what direction my life will take from here, but one thing is certain. Now I'm making more decisions with my heart. For a girl who waited fifty years for her knight in shining armor, I'm elated to have found mine. My equine teachers get full credit for patiently guiding me through the unfamiliar realm of emotions—both good and bad. Who could have predicted that Scotchie, JR, Murphy, and Sifter were setting me up to finally meet my prince charming?

—Susan Hutchinson

Grass Can Get Greener

Every morning a heavy feeling pins me to the bed. I drag myself to the breakfast table and hunch over my cereal, praying my mother won't notice my bloody cuticles.

"Tell me what's wrong!" she demands.

I can't tell her that I am a freak. That nobody at school likes me. That every gym class is a nightmare.

Two captains choose the members of their teams one by one, while I slump against the wall, praying to hear my name next. Just don't let mine be the last name called. Not that anyone cares; by the time the line dwindles to three or four rejects, the teams are already turning away and moving toward the field. Still, it is a matter of pride not to be last, and my prayer is usually granted. There is one fat girl who is apparently even more of a reject than I am.

I can't tell my kind-hearted mother that I spend recess locked in the bathroom because nobody wants to hang out with me. Terrified that somebody will notice where I am during recess, I try to convince the rotation of bodies in the other cubicles that I'm as busy as a bee in there. I calculate that the stall occupants change about six times, so I mete out my pee in order to give a convincing dribble for each occupant.

The ones who spend ages in front of the mirror really piss me off. I start to imagine they're onto me. They're going to stay out there until I am forced to emerge, and then they will identify me as the pathetic person who has to spend her recess in a smelly cubicle. But so far, so good. They leave, next one in, I start again.

But today my mother says, "Daddy and I were talking last night, and we've decided that you are old enough to look after a horse."

My heart starts to beat. "You're going to buy me a horse?"

"We've hired some men to fix up the barn a bit. We can go look at some horses on the weekend, if you'd like."

If I'd like! Even though I've been riding since the age of seven, attending Pony Club every summer, and volunteering my services at the local barn, the only thing my parents have ever said about horses is, "When will she switch her affection to boys?" And now they are offering to buy me a horse? I can't believe it!

I still can't believe it a month later when Poteet joins our family. She is a beautiful, dappled gray appaloosa, 14.2 hands high, with a scrawny mane and tail and a striking white blaze down her face. Wrinkles above her eyes give her a quizzical expression.

I love her. Every day when I get home from school I rush to the field, bestow a kiss on her forehead, and find a good spot to sit in order to sing to her. Just one kiss, because she is a snooty kind of mare and sighs when I become too passionate.

Sometimes I saddle her up, and we go for a walk in the woods. But Poteet is excitable and tends to leap about in a nerve-wracking way, so after a couple of nasty falls, I mostly just sit with her and sing. At first she ignores me, cropping grass as she moves around the field. I move after her, plunking myself down in each new spot and resuming my Beatles warble. Gradually, it seems the best grass happens to be the spot I choose to sit. As soon as I'm settled, Poteet starts to graze in my direction. Apparently, I'm hogging the most succulent piece of greenery in the whole field. But if I move, there she is again, pushing her nose under my bottom so she can flap her lips at the only blade of grass worth having.

Then I realize this is affection. I am filled with such painful delight I want to cry. I allow myself a little kiss to her eyeball, and she doesn't sigh.

Our relationship begins to grow stronger. Soon I can grab her head in a bear hug, and she won't pull away. Now it's impossible to wake up in the morning with a heavy feeling, because there's so much to laugh at before the school day starts. First, when I open the barn door, Poteet sprints down the field like she's mad, her scrawny tail high in the air. I always glance around the barn, to see if maybe it's on fire or there's a snake inside. But no, she's just being ridiculous.

I fill her feed bucket with grain and call her. She shoots back to the barn and shoulders me aside to reach the food; plunging her head in and inhaling the contents as though she's afraid I might steal them. Then she jerks her head up and looks at me, grain cascading from the sides of her mouth. She does everything in such a frenzy that I have to laugh. It's hard to leave her.

There's the whole day to plan while I'm waiting for the bus, so I don't even notice the other kids standing there. It's not like I'm ignoring them or anything—I'm just thinking about phoning the blacksmith to trim Poteet's hooves or about reminding Dad to take me to the sawmill to get more sawdust. Maybe I'll take some lessons at the local barn, so Poteet can meet other horses. There's a lot to do when you have a horse.

Recess in the bathroom isn't so bad anymore. I write to-do lists or jot down amusing anecdotes about Poteet so I can read them to her when she gets old. I don't even notice the comings and goings in the adjacent cubicles. Sometimes I just stay at my desk; it doesn't matter so much if somebody sees me by myself and thinks I don't have any friends. I do have a friend, don't I?

The vet tells me Poteet needs more exercise so I try to ride her more often. Every time we see a track leading off into the woods, we follow it to see if it evolves into a trail. The best ones are the circle trails, where you can return home without retracing your steps. Once we are comfortable with a trail, we can amble down it at leisure, but trying out a new trail for the first time is awful. Poteet rushes through unknown territory in great excitement, while my terror keeps pace with her speed. She manages to unseat me several times by veering suddenly after seeing something she considers frightening. Since she is high strung, verging on completely bonkers, she classifies many things as terrifying. So I cling to the saddle, waiting for a huge rock or an old car wreck to loom in our way. Its sudden appearance results in an abrupt about-face, and we're shooting back the same way we came. After I saw at the reins enough to finally stop her (on the rare occasions that I don't fall off), she looks back over her shoulder, sides heaving and nostrils gaping. The object in question is now a mile behind us. Once we came unexpectedly across some deer, and both Poteet and the deer leapt straight in the air and galloped in opposite directions.

A few months after I start riding on a regular basis, some kids pass us on their bikes. They all turn around to look at us, and I see that there are a couple of girls from school. My stomach feels a bit queasy, but it's nothing I can't handle.

"I didn't know you had a horse," one of them says.

"Yes. Her name is Poteet."

"Wow, you're really lucky. Can I come over and ride her someday?"

"Maybe," I say, turning onto a wooded trail where they can't follow me. Do I mean "maybe" or do I mean "go screw yourself"? Pauline has never teased me, but she hasn't been nice to me, either. She just goes along with the crowd, trying to be invisible. Like all of us.

So when she parks herself beside me at recess the next day and bombards me with questions about my "beautiful horse," I tell her she should come over and meet Poteet.

I feel a little less confident when Pauline shows up in shorts and sneakers.

"Do you know how to ride?"

"I haven't had lessons or anything but I've been on a horse," Pauline says.

My heart sinks a little. It seems to me Poteet is smiling to herself.

"Well, you pull the right rein if you want to go right, the left rein to go left, and both of them to stop."

"And I kick her to make her go forward, right?"

Poteet gives me a knowing look. "I don't think you'll have to urge her forward. Just remember how to stop."

Pauline swings up into the saddle. Poteet's ears go back flat against her head and stay there.

"Are you sure you wouldn't like me to lead you? Just at the beginning?"

"No way. I want to ride. Open the gate," Pauline commands.

"I think it's best if you just ride around the field at first."

Poteet walks sedately around the field. Pauline gives her a little kick to get her to trot and she mistakes it for a request to gallop. Poteet careens around the field. I close my eyes, but there is no thud. Pauline has a lot more guts than I had when I first rode Poteet, despite my years at the riding school. She's hanging on to the scrawny mane with both hands, and she is laughing hysterically. Poteet, disgusted with her reaction, plunges her head down to buck.

"Get her head up!" I scream. "Pull on the reins!" But Pauline lost both reins long ago, and she catapults over Poteet's head and lands smack in a pile of horse dung. Poteet stops bucking and starts to graze. I stalk over in fury, and she lifts her head in at attempt to give me a conspiratorial look. "Bad girl!" I shout, grabbing her reins and jerking them. "Bad girl!"

Pauline gets up and limps over to us, taking the reins and planting a kiss on the recalcitrant beast's nose.

"That was great," she says. "Shall we try it again?"

I come into the kitchen where Mum and Dad are having a drink.

"She doesn't bite her cuticles anymore," Mum is saying.

"Did I used to bite my cuticles?" I ask.

"It was only a year ago. Have you forgotten?"

I look down at my cuticles. They are dirty from working in the barn. "Maybe I don't bite them anymore because they're caked in horse manure. If I ever did bite them."

"I can't believe you don't remember."

"That's what children are like," says my father. "They rebound quickly."

"Are you happy now at school, sweetie?" my mother asks.

"Happy? What are you talking about? I hate school," I say cheerfully, biting into a peanut butter sandwich.

—Charlotte Mendel

One July Night

Ride On was a backyard, grassroots operation made up of folks who believed in the healing power of horses. Our assets consisted of the use of a farm just outside of town, three donated horses, and a shared sense of humor. The last one may have been the saving grace for the future of the program.

Our plans met with immediate and stern opposition from county officials before we were even up and running. They felt that they could not sanction such an activity because of the intrinsic danger in horseback riding. Furthermore, our "special equestrians," because of their physical and mental limitations, would be easy targets for lawsuits, not to mention courthouse invective in a small town. Certain pillars of the community gathered daily for lunch and railed against anything new. They wanted no part of our program in the beginning and said as much. Their attitude made us even more determined to make this work.

From the rolling hills of the farm down to the river, it was easy for us to feel optimistic about our venture. Grass was plentiful and the horses grazed the open pastures in quiet appreciation. Classy, a sunny chestnut and the veteran school horse, lifted her head and made a graceful arc with her neck, harking back to her Arab heritage. A wayward breeze teased her long mane and flowing tail as she gazed past us.

Manners, the retired gray hunter, scarcely moved. Instead, he stretched his long neck and adjusted his head under the fence in order to crop the sweet blades of grass on the other side. He had spent years going over fences and this was his well-earned reward.

Prince, a dark bay with four white stockings, was a gift from the police academy. He had been a steady mount for the officers, and we could imagine that he once cut a fine figure in parades. Large, over sixteen hands, with a noble head like that of the horses depicted on Roman coins, he had a ready look.

It would have been pure pleasure to hang on the fence all day drinking in the beauty, but we had our work cut out for us. Our first responsibility was to make sure our mounts were bombproof. We volunteers rode the horses beside the busy highway, along the railroad track, and past a construction site. We played loud music and tossed a red-and-white beach ball back and forth from the horses' backs. Cattle stared, sheep stampeded, and local dogs challenged our right to pass through their property.

Undaunted, we pressed on. At first, the morning train was a bit too much to bear for Classy and, of course, the other two horses fed off her insecurities, as horses will do. In time, all three paid little attention to the loud iron monster that roared along but kept to the track. After a week's effort, it was clear that we had three trustworthy therapy horses.

Local tack shops generously provided tack and protective headgear for the students. Halters, lead ropes, bareback pads and saddles to fit small bottoms, along with Pony Club–approved helmets in several sizes, came pouring in as soon as we put out the word. Private donations and some later fundraisers paid for insurance. Our designated attorney even won over the county officials, at least for a trial run. We had dreamed big and now it was show time.

That first night, my charge, a reedy eight-year-old girl, tore around the paddock like a wild pony, darting among the therapy horses and other special equestrians, climbing on stall doors, whooping, and resisting any contact, even by her mother. Sarah was a tangle of blonde hair and bewilderment as she ran around hitting herself rhythmically and repeating words that meant nothing to the rest of us, "Pretty flowers. Pretty flowers."

It was a sticky night in July, and the atmosphere was thick with anticipation. The volunteers assembled in the makeshift ring to saddle the horses and assist the young riders. Soon everyone was helmeted, mounted, and moving, assisted by leaders, sidewalkers, and one back rider—everyone but Sarah, who by now was screaming and slapping at her mother. Nobody knew what to do.

We were halfway through the lesson before Sarah's mother was able to diffuse the situation and lift her onto Prince, the retired police horse. Once around the ring, she was still looking back at her mother; another full turn and the magic had begun its work as Sarah relaxed into the cadence of the horse's stride, comforted. Three was a charm as she began to laugh with delight and move with the horse. Then she began to sing softly.

The arena grew quiet except for the rhythm of the hoof beats and the song without words. The music hung in the air like a Celtic flute melody, punctuated only by the child's squeals of joy. Some of us had to wipe our tears on our shirttails. Parents outside the ring stopped talking and drew nearer to marvel at what they saw. We all watched in amazement as the noble animal transformed a whirling dervish into a gentle, trusting child.

Every week thereafter was an adventure for the riders and helpers alike. We had believed in miracles, and now we expected them. Sarah became a mascot of sorts for the program, taking part in exhibitions and having her picture in the paper a lot. Her enthusiasm made believers out of skeptics wherever she went. The once-doubting county officials presented a plaque to the organization and one also to Sarah. Hers read: "You are our shining star."

Sarah stayed in the program for ten years and became an accomplished rider. She moved into a group home after her sixteenth birthday, so her parents could afford her some independence, but they stayed close enough to monitor her progress. Her two wonderful caregivers continued to bring her to weekly riding lessons. Sarah continued to live her life to the absolute fullest, following the magic that touched her on that first July night.

—Ellen Bain Smith

My Opportunity

I was driving to work in Dallas on a sunny Monday afternoon in February 1996 when I saw, out of the corner of my eye, something burgundy heading straight for my car door. The next thing I remember was the burgundy scrubs worn by the nurses in the emergency room of the local county hospital.

It had taken several hours for emergency personnel to free me from my car. Now I lay in a hospital bed with a severe brain injury that resulted in paralysis on my left side, impaired vision, hearing loss, and a host of other neurological deficits. I don't remember much about the next few weeks. All I know is that I couldn't move the left side of my body, open my jaw, or hear or see very much. I was confused and filled with fear.

Now I refer to that February day as my "opportunity."

Prior to my opportunity, I had been an internationally ranked athlete. I'd represented two countries in two sports: field hockey and squash. Born and raised in Rhodesia, now Zimbabwe, I had come to the United States in the late 1980s with only a backpack and a hundred dollars to my name. I was an independent, self-sufficient, active woman. To make ends meet, I worked several jobs—video editor, certified paramedic, neuro-linguistic programming master practitioner, and ropes challenge course instructor. In my spare time, I learned to play American sports, translated Texas English into American English, did my best to understand the game of football, learned to dance country-western style, and volunteered. I lived a fabulously full life.

After my opportunity, I spent several months at an inpatient rehabilitation facility, before graduating to an outpatient clinic. There I learned to maneuver my wheelchair using only my right arm and leg and how to dress myself with some help. Later that year I attended school five days a week for several months to relearn everything cognitive. I was like a child in kindergarten again. Every day I had to figure out how to accept the challenges that my opportunity presented to me.

After almost a year of physical, occupational, and pool therapy, my improvement reached a plateau. I had gained back some physical strength, yet still needed a lot of help with day-to-day living. Although well cared for by family and friends, I was propped up in a wheelchair with a neck brace, back brace, arm brace, and leg brace day in and day out. This once independent, self-sufficient woman was now totally dependent on others 24/7.

Then an acquaintance gave me the gift of a lifetime. She had heard about the benefits of equine therapy and gave me ten sessions at Equest Therapeutic Horsemanship, an hour from my house. I had never ridden a horse before, and I couldn't imagine what benefits I might gain from riding that I hadn't already received from conventional therapies. I knew so little about horses that when I heard a radio commercial advertising "bridal accessories and gifts for the groom," I was sure that a new tack store was opening up in my neighborhood. But despite my ignorance about all things equine, I was excited—it meant one day a week out of the house!

My family set up a transportation roster and took time off from their jobs to get me to Equest every week. The many different emotions I felt on that first day were very confusing. I was afraid, yet being around the animals brought me a sense of peace. It was wonderful to be wheeled down the aisle of the barn between the stalls with all the horses looking over their doors to see what was happening. The smell of the hay, the dusty arena, and the whinnies from these incredible animals filled my senses. What an adventure this was going to be!

Then the fear overtook me again. I sat about three feet high in my wheelchair, but my therapy horse, Mrs. B, loomed like a giant, what with my impaired vision and lack of depth perception. They wanted to put me *up there*—on that little saddle?

My coach and all the volunteers reassured me. This was *my* first time, but it was not theirs. They wheeled me up a ramp and guided Mrs. B beside my wheelchair. Three volunteers helped me into the saddle. Once seated on the little piece of shiny leather on the horse's huge, hairy back, I was more paralyzed by fear than by my injuries. I felt completely out of control. I knew I couldn't get off by myself, unless I took an "unscheduled dismount." I had no clue how to handle a horse. I'd ridden a camel once, but that experience was of no use to me now.

During that first session, and all the sessions in my first year of therapy, a volunteer walked on each side of me, holding my legs in the stirrups and stabilizing my body. A third volunteer led the horse around the arena and followed the instructor's directions. I was in awe that I, Deb Lewin, was riding a horse. I had always wanted to ride horses but never found the time to do it; so here I was, presented with this wonderful gift. Once again it confirmed for me that that February day in 1996 had indeed been my opportunity.

Gail, the head instructor at Equest, recognized that my prior, long-dormant athletic spirit could be reignited. She encouraged me to try to reach a level where I could compete against other riders with disabilities. At the same time, my doctor started to notice the benefits of my equestrian therapy: my paralyzed leg had gained back some muscle, my stomach and back muscles were stronger, I could hold my head up without a neck brace, and my confidence and self-esteem were returning. Riding horses gave me so much more than forty-five minutes out of the house. Before riding, I hadn't been able to keep my shoulders back and heels down at the same time in the eighteen months since my accident.

The physical achievements from riding trickled over into my everyday life, too. I could now hold a coffee cup in my right hand and place the cup on the counter—not drop it—to answer the phone. I regained my independence and found a new sense of freedom that changed my life for the better each and every day. Even though I was the one riding, every one of my family and friends also benefited from the therapy offered by the intuitive angels in horses' bodies.

After a few months of riding different horses and learning the beginnings of an equine discipline called dressage, Equest took several of us to compete in Missouri. We were assigned borrowed horses, practiced a little, and then competed against other riders with similar disabilities. What a rush! I'm very competitive by nature, and this was the excitement and challenge my life had been missing.

Many of the people I competed against had been riding most of their lives and owned their horses, so they could practice every day. Only recently did I realize that not everyone competes with borrowed horses. Gail reminded me, "It's the journey and not the destination," so I continued to be the best rider I could be with the horses I had. And I rode many different horses through the years, from backyard, french fry-eating ponies to huge draft horses used for vaulting. I have loved most of them.

When I got close enough to some of these beautiful horses—close enough to feel their warm breath on my face, close enough to stare into their gentle eyes, close enough to talk to them—they spoke back to me. My heart warms to these huge animals that can be so gentle and so intuitive. The look in their eyes tells me that they will take care of me. Of course, there have been a few that have wanted nothing more than to take a chunk out of me. Those are the same horses that are smart enough to realize I have no use of my left arm and leg, so they step purposefully to the left where they know I have to work very hard and use every alternate cue at my disposal to get them going straight again. When that happens, I can almost hear them chuckling.

But most of the horses do what they can to protect me. Last summer during a dressage lesson, Zena, the beautiful Arabian mare I was riding, refused to go down the long rail and kept turning toward the middle of the arena. I tried everything I could remember to get her to go straight, but nothing worked. She was adamant about not going near that end of the arena. When Gail asked me what was wrong, the image of a bunny popped into my head. I told her there was a rabbit in the far corner. Gail was skeptical. "How do you know that? You can't even see that far!" I told her that Zena had told me. When Gail approached the corner of the arena, sure enough, there was a rabbit.

Over the six years that I have been participating in therapeutic riding at Equest, my life has changed dramatically for the better. I am now an independent rider in the arena, needing only mounting and dismounting help. I have won a national equitation title and many dressage competitions, even against able-bodied riders. I am ranked among the top ten in the countryand have been selected twice for the Paralympic trials, and I represented the United States in international ParaEquestrian dressage competitions.

Although I have lost the use of part of my body, I have gained so much more through my four-legged friends and equine therapy. Thanks to Equest and all their amazing horses, I continue to ride and volunteer. I am also a motivational speaker and fervent advocate of the benefits of equestrian therapy.

I had a choice after that day of opportunity in 1996: I could focus on all the doors that had slammed shut in my face, or I could focus on the one barn door that opened for me. I chose the door that gave me back my life.

—Deborah Lewin

Learning to Laugh Again

"He's perfect," I remember telling Gary, as I petted the white blotch on Little Mister's nose.

"I agree." Gary carefully put his arm around me. "You should get him."

Mister dazzled us as he pranced around the corral with his head held high. Not even two years old, Mister had the smooth gait and stature of a

Tennessee Walker and the sensitive nature of a quarter horse. After a few times around, the trainer released the lead, and Mister walked right to me. He gave my hand a friendly lick, squealed a horsy hello, and snorted all the dust out of his nose.

Although I was still recovering from my last horse mishap and could barely turn my head, I knew Mister was the horse for me. While I wrote the check, Gary offered Mister a handful of bright green clover. As the sun sank into the trees, we drove our new purchase the sixty miles home. My heart danced with excitement like a little kid at Christmas as I thought about my new prize. "He's mine. All mine!"

Gary squeezed my hand and smiled. "It's good to see you happy again."

After we returned home, so did the reality of the concussion I had suffered two weeks earlier at my riding lesson. My head throbbed as I remembered catching my foot in the stirrup when I dismounted from Lightning, a horse I had never ridden before. He spooked and took me for an unintended and painful ride. But being the stubborn horse lover that I am, I couldn't just sit home and nurse my head or my grudge.

With cane in hand and Gary by my side, I continued my college courses, exercised, and tried to make time to see Mister. But juggling doctor appointments, classes, and Gary's work schedule didn't leave much time for the boarding stable.

For the first three months after my spill, Gary catered to my every need: he carried my books to school and drove me everywhere I had to go. Most men I know don't like driving, especially in heavy traffic, but Gary, although blind in one eye from a bout with cancer, never complained once.

Often I'd get frustrated with the aches and pains and the lack of independence. Once I threw my cane across the room. "When am I going to get back on my feet?" Gary fetched the cane, knelt down by my side, and kissed my forehead. "I know it's tough, but pretty soon you'll be riding your own horse like you used to."

My own horse! My very own horse! That's the thing that kept me going. Growing up, I'd had a horse. When Gary and I married, I moved my quarter horse, Ginger, to our new trailer house on one acre of land. But four years later, with our third child on the way, we needed something bigger than a two-bedroom mobile home. We couldn't afford a farmhouse with ample land for Ginger, so I put her up for sale. A man paid cash for her that same night. As I watched the truck pull the trailer onto the bumpy road and take her away, a part of my heart left with her. Gary knew that I hadn't been the same since.

As I raised my four children I dreamed of the day I would be able to canter through the pasture, free as the wind. After the kids grew up, we learned of Gary's cancer, so I went to work full-time to help pay the bills. When I was promoted two years later, we relocated to Houston. The transition—leaving everything behind—seemed difficult at first, but Gary, now cancer-free, had such optimism. "Everything will work out. Obviously, God must want us here. The economy is budding, and we can't complain about the weather."

Gary was right—life in Texas was better than the life we'd had in Michigan. Within the first week he found a job as an engineer. Everything our hands touched seemed to prosper. That's why it was so devastating when Gary's health deteriorated.

For the first month, we thought he had the flu. But as the illness lingered, blood tests revealed the worst—he was in the final stages of cancer. Like a wildfire out of control, it raged all through him, and there was nothing either of us could do. "I'm sorry," was all the specialists could say.

We tried chemotherapy, but Gary grew even more lethargic and bedridden. I felt so helpless. He had taken care of me, gotten me back on my feet, so why couldn't I do the same for him? I wanted so badly for him to be able to drive me to see Mister. I wanted him to put his arms around me and tell me everything was going to be okay. Before I knew what hit me, he was gone.

After the funeral, my head spun in circles. Most of the time I stayed home, wandering around the house lost and dazed. Sometimes I would wrap Gary's shirt around me and close my eyes. Inhaling the smell of his spicy aftershave in the fabric, I could pretend he was with me, holding me.

One day while I was cleaning, the front cover of a magazine caught my eye. On it was a picture of a beautiful stallion, just like Mister, standing tall and proud on his hind legs. A few minutes later I grabbed my keys and hopped in the car.

When I arrived at the stable, Mister raised his head and trotted toward the fence. I held out my hand, and he licked it just like he did on the first day we met. I pulled some clover and fed it to him. Suddenly, Mister whinnied and snorted green slime all over me. I laughed. I laughed more than I had in weeks. As I continued feeding Mister, it felt as though Gary was standing beside me. I could almost hear him say, "Boy, it's good to see you smile again."

—Elisabeth (Lisa) A. Freeman

Kayla and Music

On my first afternoon at the equine therapy barn, someone handed me a lead rope, and I took charge of a horse. And then I looked over the horse's ears at Kayla. Her pale blonde hair curled out from underneath a green safety helmet, and her seven-year-old grin was pure mischief. Born with cerebral palsy, she used a walker to get around. Riding helped strengthen her legs as she worked toward the possibility of walking on her own. I volunteered with Kayla every Tuesday and Saturday, either leading her horse or holding onto her feet, helping her stretch down and secure her weight in her stirrups. I worked with other kids and adults—lots of them—but Kayla was secretly my favorite. For months, she called me Miss Katherine, as her instructor Anita and her mother insisted, but after a while she just called me Katherine. The first time she did it she slid me a look that said she knew we were now conspirators—girls together against the adults.

After I had been at the riding center about six months, Anita asked me to take a look at a new horse. The local animal shelter didn't have facilities for horses, but they knew that our center and its compassionate staff would take care of their latest rescue. Music was a nine-year-old bay mare, intended by nature to be short and fat, but her owner had neglected her. When I first saw her, she was painfully skinny, standing as far back in her stall as she could and staring at the wall. She looked as if she was afraid to look up because she would be back where she had come from. I opened the stall door and ran my hand slowly and carefully up her neck, letting her smell me. She was perfectly content to be rubbed and petted and fed carrots; she wanted to believe in kindness, but she remained alert to the possibility of cruelty.

After Music had gained enough weight, I began staying late on Saturday afternoons to ride her around the ring. She was so nervous that it was difficult to get her to walk. She was used to impatient demands for speed followed by careless hauling back on the bit. When she learned to stand still, we began to practice the skills required of a therapy horse. I leaned forward and touched her ears, which made her a bit nervous—she was wary of sudden, even gentle, physical contact. I leaned back and touched her tail. I sat on her sideways and backwards, touched my toes, and lay down on her rump. I guided her in circles and serpentines, sat teddy bears on her withers, and tossed rings from her back. She was always eager to please and happy to slow down, but she never quite believed that this could be all I wanted.

One day as I slid off after a particularly successful ride, Anita approached me about the possibility of using Music for Kayla's riding lessons. Kayla was small, and Music was short and increasingly fat. The horse's girth would help Kayla stretch, and her height wouldn't be frightening. Also, Music's gait was short-coupled and fairly rapid, a motion that would stimulate Kayla's muscles. Years as a riding student had made Kayla occasionally lazy or uninterested. Anita thought that the challenges Music presented might keep her on her toes. Was Music ready for Kayla? I had to think about it, but finally I said I thought so, if we worked the horse before the lesson.

I bolted out of school that Tuesday and raced to the barn. By now, I could go into Music's stall at a normal pace, not pausing to let her sense my presence. She knew my smell from endless afternoon groomings, picking her tail, and rubbing her ears. The saddle and bridle posed more of a challenge, but that was as much out of normal, horsy laziness as anything. We worked in the ring for twenty minutes to get the kinks out. Then I grasped her halter, we put Kayla on her back, and I held my breath.

Kayla was excited about being allowed to ride a new horse. She also knew that Music had been abused and wanted to take care of her. As we walked along, Kayla would reach down to pat Music. I relaxed slightly, knowing that such signals would reassure the horse. It took me several more minutes to realize that Music herself was attuned to the motions of Kayla's shaky balance. When the little girl moved unsteadily, Music shifted her weight instantly. I sucked in another breath when we pulled up, and Kayla reached for Music's ears. But the horse kept her head steady, only raising it ever so slightly as her one concession to nerves. Kayla was delighted because she didn't have to reach so far. Music had clearly decided that her rider needed much more reassurance than she did, and she was determined to make things as easy as possible for Kayla.

As Kayla slid off, I rubbed Music's face affectionately. "Good job," I whispered to her. "Good girl. You did good." She closed her eyes and pushed her forehead into my hand. Usually Kayla was eager to get back to her mother's van, her little brother, and her homework. But today, as Music and I stood there waiting for her to move safely away, she came forward on her walker and stretched up her neck to give me her best puppy-dog face. "Kath-er-ine," she said, her expression telling me that she was getting ready to wheedle, "Can I help clean Music up?" Behind Kayla, I could see Anita grinning at the success of her strategy.

"Sure," I said. "You just stay near her head for a minute. We're going to take the saddle off, and then you can help me brush her at the cross-ties."

For once eager to do exactly what she was told, Kayla slid her walker next to me. "Muuuusic," she crooned, balancing on one hand and resting more weight than usual on her weak legs as she reached up to pat the velvet muzzle. The little horse was short enough for her to reach and I thought, "That's so nice. Kayla can actually pet her a little bit." No sooner had I thought it than Music, always wary of new people and strange touches, dipped her head down and gently lipped Kayla's blonde hair. Kayla laughed. "Look, Katherine!" she cried and stood up straighter to really rub between Music's eyes.

In the car on the way home, I cried. The next week, Kayla was early for her lesson for the first time I could remember. Music was harder to ride than any horse Kayla had ever ridden before. She walked faster, moved more quickly, and challenged Kayla to keep and shift her balance while paying close attention to what was going on. I worried that Kayla would lose interest, that it would get too hard, or that she would shut down and stop trying. It was hard for Kayla to use her balance and her legs; she usually refused to try to walk without her walker, and even with it, she seldom went farther than absolutely necessary. But in order to keep riding the horse, Kayla was evidently ready to work as hard as she had to, because, she told me one afternoon, Music was her friend. I believe that Kayla, after years of dependence on other people, liked the idea of taking care of someone else. Maybe Music, who had almost forgotten what it was like to be cared for, felt the same.

After Kayla and Music had been together for about six weeks, a television reporter arrived at the center to do a human-interest piece on the riding program. Immediately she seized on Kayla, who was cute as a button and posed unashamedly. "Who's your favorite horse?" the reporter asked with sugary sweetness.

"Music!" Kayla cried happily.

Anita and I shared a rueful look. The reporter was going to come back the next week with cameras, and she wanted pictures of Kayla riding her favorite horse for her story. But was Music, so new at this and so nervous, ready for prime time?

That Saturday, Music, Anita, and I went through a whole lesson. We tossed rings and circled cones and barrels. We did anything and everything that might disturb the horse, but we couldn't think of a way to reproduce the camera. We finally agreed that we would just decline any close-ups.

Tuesday afternoon I worked Music for twenty minutes before the reporter arrived. I was as nervous as I had been the very first time Kayla had ridden her. I wanted Kayla to have the thrill of riding Music on TV, and I wanted to feel the accomplishment for both of them, but I didn't want some disaster to set them both back. My stomach twisted. Carefully, I explained to the reporter that the horse had been neglected, that she was nervous, and that we were worried about the television paraphernalia. The reporter quickly agreed to no close-ups, pleased as punch with writing about the horse and the little girl who had found each other.

No sooner had we pulled into the middle of the arena where it was planned that Kayla would touch Music's ears and her tail and touch her own toes than the cameraman hustled toward us. "Please," the reporter begged from the rail, "it's just too cute, the two of them together. We just need a few close-ups."

Before I could open my mouth, the cameraman, who had clearly never been near a horse in his life, thrust his gigantic black monster up over Music's head, her most sensitive spot. The camera startled Kayla, too. I put a hand out to stop him, but it was too late. I watched Kayla, in case she needed to be taken down quickly. I clutched the lead rope, waiting for Music to back up, toss her head, or even rear up. "Poor darling, I wouldn't blame you," I thought furiously. Quickly, I looked down and into a pair of determined brown eyes. The muscles in Music's neck were tense, but she stood her ground. Nothing was going to make her disturb Kayla, who had begun to calm down.

After we had gotten rid of the reporter and her cameraman, Kayla was lifted off the horse and came around to pet her. She thrust her walker out of the way and threw her arms around the horse's neck. "Music," she said, "I love you."

"She loves you, too," I said. Kayla gave me that sly grin. "I know that," she told me contentedly and walked slowly off to talk to her mother about being a TV star.

"See that?" I asked Music, carefully leading her past the walker. "You did that."

After I had pulled the saddle off and brushed her, I threw a companionable arm over her back. "I love you," I told her.

She didn't say she loved me, too. But I knew.

—Katherine Mooney

The Drama Queen

The first part of Java that I met was her rump. It wasn't just me; that was how she greeted everyone, standing with her hind end facing the stall door and staring out the window on the opposite side at something far more interesting than you. If you're new, as I was on that first day as a volunteer at the National Center for Equine Facilitated Therapy (NCEFT), it doesn't matter how sweetly you talk or what morsels you hold in your outstretched palm; Java is just not interested.

There's nothing wrong with Java's rump; in fact, it's rather attractive. But if you were looking for a horse with perfect conformation, you would pass this particular appendix Thoroughbred by. Her back is long, her belly is round, and her legs are thin. Her neck is positioned too low and curves up like a deer's rather than nicely arching down. Her attitude is blasé when it comes to most humans. Don't bother trying to pet her or tell her what a sweet girl she is. Chitchat is not her thing.

When I started in the fall, Java was the only mare in NCEFT's string of therapy horses. There were many qualities, aside from gender, that distinguished her from the geldings. While the others display varying shades of chestnut and dun on their coarse hides, Java's coat is a lovely deep espresso and as soft as a kitten's. Her eyes shine black, her muzzle is café au lait, and there is the tiniest splash of cream on her forehead. While the guys appear by turns friendly, gluttonous, or peeved, the expression Java wears when awake is bemused. She seemed calm enough, but the horse handlers called her the "Drama Queen."

I was determined to make all the horses—including Java—my friends. Every day I carried a big bag of apple pieces, which I doled out while cooing and petting each horse admiringly. The guys had no problem signing their affection away for the price of a few tidbits. In an instant they became my new best friends for life and slobbered green goo all over me to show the depth of their love. The eyes of the Haflinger, Odie, widened as he greedily banged his stall door with a hoof and grunted like a buffalo. Golden Topaz muttered a gentle *putt-putt-putt* as he ambled to the gate. The pony Merlin squealed like a stuck pig, afraid he'd be overlooked because he's small.

Java took more convincing. She wasn't going to get all hopped up about some horse-crazy neophyte who would probably come around once or twice with treats and then be gone. But even a standoffish horse has a hard time resisting food.

While Java ignored me on that first day—and for several weeks thereafter—I noticed that she paid close attention to the horse handlers, Odette and Benedicte. Perhaps it was because they each carried a whip. Or perhaps it was because they're both Dutch. There is something about the word "Halt!" spoken with that accent that makes even the humans pull up short and await further instructions.

I soon learned that Java didn't end up at NCEFT because of her looks or her objection to small talk. She's there because she is a hard-working horse, because her personality and temperament are uniquely suited to therapy work, and because she's smart—maybe too smart. And she's there because she has a sense of humor.

Five-year-old Hayley rides Java on Tuesdays. Cerebral palsy limits her movements and flexibility, but her impishness punctuates the therapy sessions with giggles and questions. One day she asked what Java did before she came to NCEFT. Odette, who was driving Java with long lines, said that she thought she had once been a polo pony. All of us—sidewalkers, therapist, and patient alike—looked at Java with surprise. Could a slow-moving, gentle therapy horse have once been an equine athlete? Java's black eyes gleamed in the shaded arena. She didn't say.

Later, I found one tantalizing hint to Java's former life in a curled photograph pinned up in the tack room. It showed a fit brown horse galloping with a rider through the underbrush. I was told the horse was Java and the rider was her former owner, Barb, but it was hard to believe that it was the same calm, brown mare that has perfected the Power Nap. Tacked up and left alone for thirty seconds, Java's eyes close, her lower lip quivers, and her head droops lower and lower until she's supporting its weight on her mouth against the side reins. "Out on the trail, she'll go all day," said Benedicte, who exercises Java in the mornings. This horse seemed to have a split personality.

Buried in a bent metal file cabinet was Java's Jockey Club registration. Cance, as she was christened at birth, was twenty years old. Any accomplishments by her parents, Stow the Throne and Doc's Mathilda, were lost to history, as was any record of Cance's first few years. They weren't all sweet hay and clover, however, and the polo career seemed doubtful. In 1992, a woman spotted Cance and her sister neglected and starving in a field. In their hunger, the horses had chewed off each other's tails, but Cance, undaunted and optimistic, was entertaining herself by jumping assorted obstacles.

The woman bought both horses on the spot, and posted Cance for sale on a grocery store bulletin board. A university professor bought the horse and renamed her Zsa Zsa. She was thrilled to find a Thoroughbred—even a fake one—for such a low price. But the two never developed the chemistry that every rider looks for in that one perfect horse. The professor found

Zsa Zsa pokey, stubborn, and aloof. In spite of the hardships she had endured, Java's queenly reserve and sense of entitlement, as well as her ability to amuse herself, remained intact. The professor offered to donate Zsa Zsa to NCEFT, where she knew the horse would get first-rate care. But Barb, the facility's director at the time, bought her instead and renamed her Java.

Java is a one-woman horse, and that woman is Barb. At last, horse and rider had found their soul mates. Barb rode Java for six years and trained her to be a therapy horse. Java was the hardest to train of any horse she had ever worked with. Some horses take a week, others take a few months, but Java took six months, and it was another two years before she took on a full schedule of patients.

When Barb's life took her back to her native Australia, it was difficult to leave Java behind, but she knew that NCEFT was the horse's home now. Java was meant to do this job that she was good at and enjoyed. On Barb's infrequent visits back to the States, the bond between her and Java is obvious. Only for Barb will Java come when called and put up with all manner of chitchat. Only for Barb does she emit a low, rumbly nicker of greeting. Everyone else gets her rump.

By my fifth or sixth week of volunteering, my persistence began to win Java over. At the sound of my voice, she would slowly swing herself around and examine me. Unlike the guys, Java didn't beg—she would never stoop that low. If someone decides to give her a treat—which she deserves, thank you very much—she will humor that someone by deigning to accept it. We stared at each other, Java chewing thoughtfully, head just out of arm's reach, confident that, yes, she did, indeed, deserve a treat.

Another of Java's Tuesday riders is five-year-old Lisa, a spindly girl who seems to be made out of rubber bands. Every week, she wears a different jacket trimmed with flowers, beads, or faux leopard skin. Despite her impaired vision, Lisa is a natural rider, sitting with perfect posture, feet in the stirrups, back straight, head up, and moving easily with the rhythm of the horse. In an instant, she can kneel, turn around to face backwards, or stand up while Java continues her steady pace.

That pace is what makes Java such a good therapy horse. It is extremely smooth, rhythmic, and gradable. She can adjust her pace to be painstakingly slow to accommodate patients who can't handle much movement, or she can lengthen it to challenge higher-level patients—all while maintaining a particular kind of motion, whether side-to-side, forward and back, or diagonal. Java knows when her rider can't deal with any shenanigans and walks as if on eggshells. Her head stays lowered, her level of focus measured in drips of saliva and the flapping of her lower lip. Despite her difficult training, Java turned out to be one of the most versatile therapy horses anyone had ever seen. Her flexibility allows the NCEFT therapists to use her in many different ways and with a variety of patients. In 2003, Java's versatility earned her the first Horse of the Year Award given by the American Hippotherapy Association. And she truly enjoys her work. Tacked up and turned loose, she will walk to the mounting block and align herself perfectly.

As a sidewalker, my view of Java is limited and usually of her off side. With my hand or arm positioned to steady the rider, I catch glimpses of Java's deeply angled pasterns. I look at her right eye. Even though I'm walking alongside her ribs, I know she can see me just as well as I can see her. I watch her long, pointed ears as they swivel to listen to the child on her back, her driver, or a bird in the bushes. If a horse can have a look of studious concentration, she has it.

One Tuesday, I finally saw for myself why Java was called the Drama Queen. Ten minutes before her next session, Odette opened her stall to tack her up. There Java lay, flat on her side, eyes rolling, tongue lolling, and a weird equine grin on her lips. When Java was new to the program, this display provoked frantic calls to the vet. Today, Odette tugged on the halter and chastised the horse in a mock-angry tone made even more menacing by her accent. "Lieve schat, wordt wakker! Als het niet teveel moeite is, zou je dan misschien je benen onder je lichaam kunnen zetten. Plaats jezelf in het land van de wakkere paarden!" I took a step back.

Unbeknownst to me, it was all a big show, and Java, who apparently understands Dutch perfectly, was playing along with the gag. Odette was merely telling her to get up and put herself "in the land of the awake horses." I don't understand Dutch, so I asked, "If she were really sick, she'd be groaning, wouldn't she?" Right on cue, Java let out a pathetic "Uuunnnhhhhhhh!" Our burst of laughter gave her all the satisfaction she needed. Performance over, a moment later she was up and ready for work. It was probably that very same sense of fun that kept her alive when she was abandoned and nearly starved all those years ago.

Three-year-old Grace is Java's last Tuesday patient. She always arrives early for her session so her father can hold her up on the rough wooden railing that surrounds the arena. She stands next to Java, who is tacked up and dozing. A smile dimples the girl's cheeks, and her green eyes fill with happiness as she visits with "her" horse. Grace can hardly wait to get on. Her leg muscles are stiffened by cerebral palsy, but periodically she leans forward as far as she can to pat Java's soft neck.

One spring day after the end of the last session, all the patients, volunteers, and staff left the ring so Java could roll. She walked with her nose to the ground to the center of the arena. When she found the right spot, she folded her slender legs, rolled onto her back, and thrashed her hooves in the air. Unlike some horses, Java can roll completely over. After a couple of good turns, she hoisted herself up, shook herself off, and with a squeal and a jump galloped to the rail, looking for all the world as if she would leap over it. Stopping just shy, she gazed out at the paddock where Odie dozed. Excitement over for the day, she let the halter be slipped over her head and walked back to her stall for the night.

After a year of bringing apples once a week, all the horses now recognize me as the Apple Lady. The first one to see me sets off the alarm, and soon they all clamor for their share. Even Java now waits expectantly near her stall door, although she never utters a sound.

One day she showed me her coy side. As I worked my way to each stall, she watched me carefully from the far end of the barn. When I turned and addressed her directly, she immediately looked away. It wouldn't have surprised me if she had started whistling. She was anxious for her treats but determined that she never be *seen* to be so. When I moved to pet her, she didn't lift her head out of arm's reach. Perhaps I'd earned the right since I brought her such delicious morsels. I did not just show up once and leave. I felt as though this queenly equine had bestowed upon me the greatest honor she could: her tolerance.

One afternoon, Java was brushed and tacked up to work with her two o'clock patient for half an hour before being untacked and put back in her stall. Because we were one volunteer short, there was no time to waste when we hurried to get her for her three o'clock session. We looked into her stall. There she lay, legs tucked neatly under her, blinking her beautiful dark eyes. She made no move to budge.

"Come on, Java! Let's go, girl!" Benedicte sang as she slid open the door, halter in hand. Java stared. Just as Benedicte came within a foot of the mare, Java eased over on her right side and flailed her thin legs in the air. She rolled partway up, looked first at Benedicte, then at me, and leaned back over again. Content that she had accomplished her goal, she stood up and marched amiably out the door, completely covered in clingy curls of wood shavings, which, of course, would have to be brushed off her before she could be retacked. As she strode past, I could have sworn that horse winked at me.

—A. Bronwyn Llewellyn

He Cried My Tears

I held my hand in front of me, unable to perceive its shape, size, color, or dimensions. The reality of my blindness shattered my heart. Like a candle blown out by an unexpected draft, my self-confidence, motivation, and purpose disappeared, leaving my world as shapeless as a lump of wax. In the turmoil of my sorrow, only the pleasant memories of my best friend momentarily dispelled my heart's darkness.

"I got something for you, honey," announced Daddy in a singing tone one day when I was eleven years old and sick in bed with the flu. His deep but tender voice always caressed my heart with comfort. And this announcement made it beat a little faster.

He carried the most beautiful saddle I'd ever seen. It was bright red and black with brilliant diamond cutouts around the rim. Its sparkle brightened my room, and the scent of fresh leather filled the air. Daddy placed it at the foot of the bed. I pushed aside the covers, sprang to my feet, and ran my fingers slowly across the cool, slick seat for the first time. I looked up at Daddy and beamed.

He smiled. "Do you like it?" He knew a gift for my four-legged friend, Scout, pleased me more than a gift for me. "I guess even the flu can't keep you from a new present," he laughed and bounced the empty saddle on the bed, mimicking a bucking horse. The bright, new saddle seemed to make my flu symptoms disappear.

"Scout will love this," I said to myself as I carried the treasure out the next day. Scout seemed weak and scared when I came into the dark barn. I found him in the back stall, hiding in a shadowed corner. As soon as I saw him, I quickened my steps. I could feel the soft dirt under my feet and smell the strong odor of wet hay. I drew closer and whispered, "Hey boy, look what I have for you!" I swung the saddle up and positioned it on his back. I took a step back to observe his reaction. His wiry legs looked stronger. He held his head higher and looked from side to side with pride. The colors of the saddle accented his shiny, dark brown hide. He was no longer a scrawny, skinny, and scared horse; he was now a strong, radiant warrior ready to defend a kingdom in battle.

When we spent precious moments together, Scout became my warrior, my defender, and my confidant. Countless rides over familiar paths became our routine, and he grew to know me better than I knew myself. The passing years took away some of the radiance of that new saddle, but our relationship continued to smooth and deepen just like its beautiful leather. Even at seventeen, I shared my fears and joy only with Scout. No one else listened the way he did.

One afternoon as Scout grazed peacefully, sun rays stroking his hide and a soft breeze lifting his mane, my world shook violently. The ophthalmologist said, "There is no cure for this retinal disease." I sank in the chair, hoping he would offer some words of hope, but he followed his diagnosis with more dark news. "I'm afraid it will eventually take her sight. It's only a matter of time." He spoke to Daddy while I listened in horror. We rode home in silence. Daddy offered his loving comments, but this time none of them drew a smile from me.

Each passing day brought painful evidence of my diminishing peripheral vision. The retinal condition dimmed the light in my world and darkened my emotional life as well. As my eyesight faded, so did my desire to participate in all the activities that I had loved before. A maelstrom of conflicting feelings flogged my heart.

"Do you need any help picking out your clothes?" Daddy asked in a soft voice one day.

"No, I can do it myself!" I shouted back, unfairly venting my frustration at him. After he quietly walked out, I threw my clothes down, flung myself on the bed, and sobbed and sobbed. I could no longer distinguish colors or shapes. Coordinating my clothes, a task I used to perform with pleasure and ease, was now impossible.

"Anytime you need to go anywhere, just let us know," friends offered. "You know we're here for you," they would add in a compassionate tone. They expressed support, but they couldn't know what I felt in my heart. I only shared the intensity of my fear, anguish, and frustration with Scout. When I cried into his neck, he nickered softly and nuzzled my shoulder with his velvet nose. I sensed his tenderness when I offered up my deepest pain and desperate longing as my life sank into a dark tunnel. *I'll be here for you. I'll be your eyes,* he seemed to say.

Scout was protective of his sightless rider as he galloped more cautiously. Unable to direct his path, I couldn't guide him around dangerous obstacles. But I trusted him. And he proved more than capable, not only at carrying me around physical dangers, but also at easing me through devastating emotional pitfalls. His protective nature emerged with anyone or anything that threatened to harm me. No one else seemed to know how to take away the sting of living a sightless life. With each ride, he gave me joy, helping me forget my heart's burdens for a while.

When my friends made plans to see a movie, they added, "You can go too if you want."

"No, that's okay, I'll just go home," I replied quickly. With tears rolling down my cheeks, I made my way across the grass, following the sounds coming from the barn. I found the stall where my loyal friend waited and hugged his muscular neck, feeling the warmth of his body. Scout stood still, listening to my sobbing whispers. He understood more than just my words. Gratefully, I stroked his face with palms wet from my tears. He seemed to cry with me, *You're not alone, I'm hurting too.*

When the time came for me to leave home for college, Daddy parked the car alongside the fence so Scout could put his head through my window. As I hugged his neck, our tears mingled once again. We didn't need words. Like the beautiful saddle I had once placed on his scrawny back, he placed a shining glow of compassion and love on my broken world. Our hearts were forever braided together in a rope of unconditional love. He became my eyes, allowing me to see what sighted people could not. Even when I was unable to express my own darkest feelings, he read my heart, sensed my pain, and cried my tears.

—Janet Eckles

Some Things I Won't Give Up

Rheumatoid arthritis is a disease of deprivation; it takes away many things that I take pride in. I give them up to ease the pain, and to free myself to have the energy to do the things that I still can accomplish. Most things I accept; some I won't.

We live on a cattle ranch, where I've always taken part in the outdoor work and ridden with the cowboys. Our babies rode in front of me until they were three and could ride their own horses—cow horses that took over their training. Still, I rode close by. We took the easy jobs: watching an open gate, pushing slow cows. It was a lesser job, but I was on a horse. When the child no longer needed close supervision, I became a cowboy.

When I reached fifty, rheumatoid arthritis and an old knee injury caught up with me. First I walked with a cane, then an arm crutch, and finally two crutches. I gave up vacuum cleaners, mops, and things that hurt my pride. I gave up things that made me feel like a contributing member of society. But I would not give up riding. My horse and I had grown old together and compensated for each other's foibles. How could I give him up?

Copper Doc was not your typical stallion. He helped raise my seven kids. He babysat them when they were three and taught them to rope when they were eight. Now, like me, stiff joints and short energy slowed his pace, but we still liked to get out.

Copper Doc's pasture gate was near my back door. I'd call, and he'd come slide his nose into the open halter. He followed behind my crutches. There was barely room for both of us in the crowded tack room as I slid my light English saddle onto his back. Outside I would lay my crutches in the back of the pickup, step on the trailer hitch, and pull myself up by the tailgate to the bumper. Copper Doc would stand against the truck and wait as I wallowed onto his back. I'd leave the reins slack as I turned him toward the creek, signaling a mutual adventure.

My world expanded when I was astride the horse. Copper Doc's strength flowed through my legs and made me whole again. He walked where I no longer could. We plowed through rough sagebrush. He splashed through the creek and followed the trail through the cottonwoods. Deer jumped in front of us. We inspected the beaver's work as water cascaded over its dam. The old horse and I needed this short trip back in time.

Out in the meadow, Copper Doc lifted his head and flared his nostrils. Did he smell mares on the breeze? His chest swelled as he moved slowly, building speed until he stretched out and ran. Joy filled my soul and released me from my earthly body. We ran free, suspended in memories of happy times.

A black cloud appeared from nowhere, building in size and depth, but I couldn't break the spell of the run. The storm hit with wind-slashed sleet and hail. Copper Doc stopped and turned tail to the cloudburst. I lay on his neck and buried my face in his mane, stealing his warmth, acknowledging his wisdom. The storm was over almost before it began. My wet clothes sharpened my awareness of the day. We rode back to the barn.

November's snow-laden winds moved Copper Doc back to his warm barn, and I went to the hospital for a knee replacement. Home again, I watched him sun himself in his corral. The snow retreated from the green grass as the bend came back in my knee. Copper Doc smelled spring as the cowboys trailed his twenty mares past his corral. Did he realize a new stallion reigned over this band? I made sure one old mare and colt would always live in his field behind the house.

I went back to the barn the next day. This time, my husband saddled my horse and helped me onto the pickup bumper. He held Copper Doc tight against the truck while I slid on. The old feelings rushed over me. Copper Doc's strength again flowed up through my legs and filled my body. There was no stiffness or pain. No feeling of being closed in and restrained. As Copper Doc moved off, his body shifted to balance me. Unsteady as I was, I felt safe on his back. As we turned toward the meadow the birds sang and the earth smelled of spring and birth and growing things. We followed the trail through the trees as raucous birds quarreled over their territory. Deer stood motionless in the shadows. The creek churned with melting snow and tumbled over mended beaver dams.

Now, two years later, my leg is strong, and the arthritis is under control, but time has taken my friend. Without Copper Doc, I'm afraid to ride. The ranch horses are eager to work and spook at shadows. I miss the old friend who took care of me.

Our two sons now run the ranch.. When they need extra cowboys, they come to our house with the loaded horse trailer. Tom's rope horse, Scooter, has my saddle. The horse is fast and quick, but he has a kind heart and doesn't mind looking after a stiff old lady. Sometimes I'm tired and depressed and think I'll stay home, but the boys look so pleased when I go. They know my heart craves a horse.

I lead Scooter beside the trailer's running board. He, too, stands patiently while I climb on. Scooter steps out and his strength flows up through my legs. We ride off and his body shifts under me, balancing, reassuring. We do the easy jobs, watching an open gate, pushing the slow cows. We ride across the meadow and through the creek. We watch deer and beaver and smell the warm earth. There is no fear. My heart sings with freedom and the beauty of the day. I've given up many things. Some things I won't.

—Mary Hadley

Yoga for Two

A *wild whinny split the air* as I entered the barn where I planned to board Vida, my new mare. The previous owners had dropped her off earlier, and I couldn't wait to saddle her up. Vida had been advertised as a push-button horse, perfect for a not-quite beginner like me. My lifelong dream of owning a horse had at last come true.

"Good morning," I said as she thrust her beautiful chestnut head over the stall half-door. I reached out to stroke the white blaze that ran the length of her nose.

Vida backed away from my hand, tossed her head, and whinnied again. She had nervously scattered her dinner and breakfast hay all around the stall that was to be her new home. From the far wall, she faced me squarely and raised one front leg as if to paw the ground, then lifted it higher so that she pawed the air over and over. This wasn't part of my dream. She had seemed relaxed in her former corral where I briefly rode her before writing the check that made her mine. If she was a push-button horse, where was the button to settle her down? I couldn't imagine going into the stall to put on her halter, let alone riding her.

Vida was half Arab. I knew Arabians were usually spirited, but in all my trips to friends' barns, I'd never seen such an anxious horse. Yet I had to smile in spite of my fear. I doubted that she had ever seen a more anxious owner. Several years earlier I'd been diagnosed with Post-Traumatic Stress Disorder (PTSD) after memories of childhood abuse abruptly surfaced. Anxiety topped the list of symptoms. Some people say horses mirror their owners. If that's true, we were perfect for each other.

"You'll be okay," I said, but my shaky voice failed to convince either one of us. She shifted her weight and pawed the air with her other front leg. "I'll give you a treat if you come here." I held out a carrot I'd brought along as a get-acquainted gift. She looked at it, put both front hooves on the ground, and her wary eyes softened a little. But she didn't budge.

"The world is a damn scary place, isn't it," I said, so interested in her fear that for a moment I forgot my own. I slipped into the stall. She tossed her head, took another step backward, and rolled her eyes so they showed white.

"Have it your way," I said, tossing the carrot in her feed pan and moving back into the arena. If the owner of the barn or other boarders had been around, I would have asked their advice for dealing with Vida's frenzied behavior. I considered calling her former owners and canceling the sale. "But," I thought, "what if my friends and husband turned their backs on me whenever I had a panic attack?"

Over the next few days, I phoned my horse-savvy friends for advice. One referred me to a trainer and instructor, Laura, who agreed to give me riding lessons. She showed me techniques I could use to quiet Vida as I entered her stall and put on her halter. She taught me to circle Vida on a long line to further calm her, and to begin every ride moving in serpentines that relaxed her chronically tense neck.

Chiropractic work revealed that Vida's back and ribs were extremely tender, perhaps from a saddle that had cut into her shoulders or distributed weight unevenly. Laura helped me try a dozen saddles before I found one that fit. I brushed and lightly massaged Vida and carefully saddled her before every ride, taking several minutes to cinch her up. Occasionally, I drove the twenty-five-minutes to the barn, not to ride at all but to simply visit with her and build her trust in me.

All those trips to the barn made me think hard about my priorities. When had I ever taken this much time and gone to this much expense to make myself physically comfortable? I, too, carried an inordinate amount of tension in my shoulders and back. I had better do something about it at last. I enrolled in a yoga class and began to do some of the poses at home so that I, like Vida, could relax and gain more flexibility.

Progress came in baby steps for both of us. When I rode, I held the reins more quietly, and gradually my legs relaxed against Vida's sides. As Vida's back grew stronger, her trot grew lighter and springier. But it still sometimes took forty-five minutes to catch her in the ten-acre pasture. And when I cinched her up, she often whipped her head around, teeth bared. When we cantered or galloped on trail rides with friends, she would spook sideways at shadows and strange noises, once unseating me. She felt like a coiled spring.

I wondered about my beautiful but difficult horse. I understood why I was such an anxious person, but why was Vida so high strung? Was it simply her personality? Did she have physical limitations we hadn't yet diagnosed? Had something happened to her? The previous owner claimed not to know what caused the scar on her shoulder. Had some event created an emotional scar as well as a physical one? She had a desperate desire to please. If I scolded her with a loud, angry voice during groundwork, she backed away, trembling. If I barked orders or abruptly dug in my heels while I rode her, she startled. Did she have an inner critic as fierce as mine?

Still, I loved her more and more.

One day during a lesson, Vida stalled and tossed her head. No matter how I cued her with the reins or my legs, she refused to transition from a walk to a trot. Discouraged, I dismounted and asked Laura to ride her. As Laura lifted a toe to the stirrup, Vida swung her head around, snapped, and somehow caught my thumb. I yelped and grabbed my hand. When Laura faced Vida and scolded her, Vida threw up her head and jumped backward, losing her balance and falling into a stall doorway.

Vida screamed in such pain that my breath stopped in my throat. For a few moments, she bucked frantically around the ring. I watched, terrified, as Laura finally brought her to a standstill. Vida stood shaking and sweating profusely. Her entire hind end had dropped to an angle neither Laura nor I had ever seen. I quickly unbuckled the girth and eased the saddle from her back, then ran to the house to call the vet. When I returned, Vida was lying on the ground, still trembling and sweating. I expected her to die before my eyes.

The vet came and administered enough pain medication to get Vida on her feet. She would live, but she had torn all the ligaments between her sacrum and pelvis. Her healing depended on physical therapy. Riding her was out of the question for the foreseeable future. The issue was no longer what I wanted her to do and how I should ask, but rather what she was able to do and how I could best assist her.

I enlisted the help of Missy, another instructor and trainer who also did a lot of equine body work. She taught me to listen to an ear twitch, a muscle spasm, or a change in breathing as I practiced techniques of massage, cranial-sacral adjustments, and energy work that would treat emotional as well as physical problems. Three to four times a week, I did the stretches with Vida that the vet had given me, as well as some Missy added. Much of the work I did with Vida reminded me of my yoga practice. Once afraid to stretch her hind legs, I now raised a back hoof, supported the lower leg, and lifted it to raise the hip. I held it for a few moments, then extended the leg forward and toward the midline.

"Think of this as a variation on warrior pose," I told her.

With practice, I became comfortable handling every part of her thousand-pound body. I would stand with my nose almost against hers, blowing into her wide nostrils and murmuring words of love and encouragement. She would respond with a nuzzle or her own soft, warm breath.

As I listened more acutely to Vida's body, I became better able to monitor my own physical reactions to stress. I enrolled in a second weekly yoga class, added more home practice, and treated myself to an occasional massage. Working with Vida was my meditation. In her company, I was temporarily freed from my own relentless anxiety.

For six months after her accident, I only did stretches and body work with Vida. Eventually I led her on walks, first five minutes, then fifteen, then half an hour. As I accepted the fact that her healing would require time, I recognized my impatience with my own healing. It, too, would take time. I tried to give myself some of the same gentle encouragement I gave to Vida.

The vet warned me that scar tissue wouldn't have the flexibility of normal tissue and Vida would have impaired range of motion. Similarly, I had been told my PTSD could easily trigger serious physical disease, and my emotional life might inhibit any normal social functioning. But Missy and I firmly believed that it's possible to heal every cell of a body and every facet of an emotional life—equine or human. I refused to accept the vet's—or my own doctor's—prognosis.

Finally I rode Vida again. Missy became my riding instructor. She worked with me to teach Vida how to relax her jaw and bend her neck so that she could respond to the slightest pressure of the bit. We worked on physical conditioning so Vida could remain collected and relaxed at the same time, tucking her nose, shortening her back, and engaging her hindquarters for forward movement and fluid transitions. As we healed Vida's injuries from the accident, we also addressed the problems she had brought with her from her two previous homes.

Vida has now invented her own stretches to add to ours. I laugh as she extends her neck and, at the same time, stretches one hind leg behind her. Or she may turn her head to one side while lifting the opposite hip. I do dog pose in my yoga classes. She does "horse pose."

Two years after the accident, she often walks up to me in the pasture when I call her name. Occasionally she waves a leg at me, and I try to decode her message. The waving leg might mean something is stiff and sore; it might be that one of her buddies has moved to a new barn, and she's grieving; or it could mean that a new horse has joined the herd, creating the stress of adjusting to a different herd hierarchy. As I brush her, comb her mane and tail, stretch her legs and neck, or "iron" her ribs, I tell her what is worrying me most at the moment. Her liquid eyes look at me, and sometimes she nudges my arm in sympathy or lays her head on my shoulder. Week by week, month by month, my yoga horse and I are healing together.

—Samantha Ducloux Waltz with Melissa Farmer

Getting to Know Blackie

On a warm, sunny morning in early June, I drove my van down a winding gravel driveway until a faded red barn came into view. I could see horses grazing peacefully in pastures and one paddock where a spirited black horse was being exercised. "Look, Allie," I said brightly. "You're going to ride on a real horse!"

It was our first visit to Saddle Pals, the therapeutic horseback-riding program for people with disabilities. After waiting on a list for months, my three-year-old daughter had finally been selected as a new rider. Allie had been in and out of hospitals for much of her short life. Born with Down syndrome and severe heart problems, she spoke little, preferring to use sign language. I thought Saddle Pals would offer her a wonderful chance to exercise outdoors in the fresh air. When I'd called, the staff had assured me that Allie's balance, strength, and endurance would improve as she rode the specially trained horses.

"Go home," Allie signed firmly with her little fingers. "Rude place. Go home now."

"No, it's a nice place," I coaxed. "You'll ride a little pony and have fun here." I gave her a reassuring smile and pointed toward the horses. Allie glared balefully at me from under her blonde bangs.

"No way," she signed fiercely before folding her arms and scrunching down in her seat.

Taking a deep breath, I lifted my uncooperative daughter out of the van and sat her down on the gravel path. She dragged her feet and lagged behind as we walked into the dimly lit barn.

Horses poked their noses inquisitively over the half-doors of the stalls. Volunteers in riding breeches and T-shirts greeted us warmly, but Allie turned her head away in silence. "What a wonderful place," I thought to myself. "Allie will love the horses and these friendly people."

Allie, however, clearly had other thoughts. The barn was dusty and filled with strange sounds and smells. Frantically she signed, "Bad horses. Allie no want. No more horse!" She stopped suddenly and cried out in alarm when a chestnut mare poked her head over the half-door and snorted loudly. A young woman bustled over to us.

"I'm Meg. I'll be working with Allison today." Holding out a small white helmet, she added, "Allison, you must put this on. It will keep you from getting hurt if you fall off the horse."

"Hat go away!" Allie signed in alarm. "No fall. No horse!" The instructor quickly put the helmet on Allie's little head and strapped it firmly in place. A volunteer led us over to Blackie, an adorable, plump pony waiting patiently beside the mounting block. Peering inquisitively at the little girl, Blackie planted his sturdy hooves, flicked his tail at the buzzing flies, and waited for the instructor's commands. Allie, however, was clearly terrified of this ferocious animal. "Horse big," she signed. "Fall off! Fall off!" The instructor persevered and Allie spent sixty miserable minutes riding around the arena. Three volunteers struggled to keep the wiggling, screaming girl on top of the pony as he plodded slowly onward. Blackie seemed a bit puzzled by the commotion, but he played his role with great dignity and kept his gait steady.

The hour seemed interminable, but finally Allie and her entourage returned through the gate to the mounting block. Exhausted and terrified, she signed "Bye-bye" to the staff. She sobbed all the way home, signing emphatically, "No more horse!"

Week after week, we traveled that same winding driveway to Saddle Pals. Crying and clutching Blackie's mane, Allie resisted all efforts to gain her cooperation. As we left the stable, she would grip my hand and sign, "Home now, no more horse!"

One day we saw a stranger in the barn. A tall, lean man in his seventies leaned casually against one of the stalls. Catching sight of the dejected child, he smiled warmly and moved slowly toward us. Allie peered at him with interest from her hiding spot behind my legs. Slowly the man lowered his denim-clad knees to the dirt floor. Silently he waited until Allie took a tentative step in his direction.

"Hello," he said, tipping back his battered cowboy hat. "I'm Grover. Are you ready to ride on Blackie today?" They gazed at each other for a long moment, blue eyes meeting blue eyes in a special, secret communication. Allie slowly reached out one hand and touched Grover's cheek. She stroked his lined face and tentatively fingered his hat. Ever so slowly, Grover extended his hand, and she grasped it firmly in her own. She gave the faintest of nods as she looked down at her canvas sneakers. Grover stood up and brushed the dirt off his jeans. Together they walked slowly over to the mounting block.

Grover whispered softly into Allie's ear as another volunteer brought Blackie around. Finally, he tenderly lifted Allie onto the saddle blanket. I held my breath, waiting for the inevitable screams. Blackie trudged slowly to the arena with Allie perched awkwardly—silently—on his broad back. Grover kept pace at her side, patting her leg and smiling. Tears came to my eyes as Allie cautiously raised her hands to sign, "Friend horse. Wait, Mom," before turning back to Grover.

For the next hour, Allie flirted with Grover as Blackie walked. When the lesson was over, Allie and Grover came back through the gate hand in hand, leading the ever-patient Blackie. "I busy, Mom," Allie signed as she toddled past the bench where I sat.

With Grover's guidance, she brushed her little pony and patted his side to thank him for the wonderful ride.

Today, Allie is a poised five-year-old who rides confidently around that same arena. She sits tall in her saddle, feet in the stirrups, and reins held tightly in both hands. "Walk on," she tells Blackie in hard-won words. Allie and Blackie have accumulated many ribbons and trophies in special-needs horse shows, and she now eagerly anticipates her weekly lesson.

One memorable evening last winter, Allie and I dressed in our best clothes to speak at a fundraising dinner for Saddle Pals. Men and women in glittering evening dress filled the elegant country club dining room. Allie stood at my side as I spoke at the podium after dinner. Suddenly she tired of waiting and headed back to our table. Halfway across the floor, she paused uncertainly, bewildered in the crowded room. Suddenly, a tall figure rose and held out his arms. "Come to Grover, Allie." With a cry of joy, she ran across the room to her trusted friend. Safe in his welcoming arms, she smiled at the applause from the audience. "Grover and Blackie," she crowed. "Go ride Blackie!"

—Sandy Keefe

One Horse, Two Transformations

DANIE'S STORY

When I bought Unaweep Bar, I was in the middle of a very difficult marriage. I was already a trainer of reining horses, but I also wanted to show them. My husband kept telling me I wasn't any good, and one horse I'd been working with seemed to be proving him right. The horse was difficult, distracted, full of himself, and ornery. Whatever I wanted him to do, he would do the opposite. Ultimately, I knew he wouldn't work in competition.

I heard Unaweep was for sale, went to try her in Walden, Colorado, and bought her. I soon realized that she tried hard, and she was very talented. She picked up maneuvers that other horses took months to learn. She was also easy to work with, except that the arena upset her—the confinement made her feel trapped. She had grown up in the mountains, so I decided to take her back to her familiar territory and ride the trails. I wanted to get away from my stressful marriage anyway, and the daytrips into the mountains provided a good excuse. Unaweep was calm and happy from the moment I unloaded her in the open terrain. As she loped, slow and relaxed, I realized that back home, *both* of us felt trapped.

As Unaweep learned to relax and trust me in the arena, she validated my skills as a trainer. She also corroborated the truth about my husband. He was always telling me that if I were a better trainer I would win more, we could get more horses in training, we'd have more money, and our life would be better. It was all my fault. Unaweep didn't like him. She had a timid personality anyway, but she wouldn't even let him ride her, which only made him more angry.

I hadn't realized how hard my husband was on me until I began a course in mental toughness for riders. I needed the training in order to compete on Unaweep, but it also showed me that I had to be mentally tough with my husband. During the course, I realized that I had to stop beating myself up.

Positive phrases helped. Realizing how negative I was made me see how much my husband's attitude had hurt me.

Meanwhile, Unaweep and I experienced something honest and true. Her timidity made me calmer. As I rode, I learned to leave thoughts of my marriage behind and be quiet and peaceful. I also became more protective of Unaweep. I wouldn't let my husband be mean to her. I knew the ugly things he said about her weren't true. He constantly told me that I wasn't good enough to compete, but at shows other people would tell me how nice Unaweep and I looked and how well she was going. In one show, we were leading in two divisions, but my husband still found negative things to say. I knew then that the problem wasn't with me or the horse—the problem was him. I soon realized that if I could stick up for her, I could stick up for myself.

Without her knowing it, Unaweep made my life easier. I had almost come to believe that everything bad in my marriage was my fault. I grew to understand that what my husband and I had was not a giving relationship or a nice place to be. When I felt Unaweep's responsiveness, I realized that partners should be caring and protective of one another, and that some partnerships *did* work. The better rider I became on her, the more positive I became about my life, and the more threatened my husband felt. I wouldn't work with a dangerous horse that wanted to hurt me, and I decided that I didn't want to be in a marriage that was hurting me. Eventually I reached the day when I could tell my husband, "We're not what you say we are," and I left.

Later, when I was happily remarried, I bred Unaweep and she had three foals. One day my husband told me we needed to sell her because she was nearly fourteen, and we weren't going to breed her anymore. I knew he was right. By then my business was thriving. In order to be competitive on my other horses, I didn't have time to work with Unaweep. Still, with our bond and our history—she had healed me in many ways—it was difficult to think about giving her up. Something inside me kept asking, "Why are you being so stubborn?" I prayed about it. I loved her and wanted the best for her. Could there be someone else who needed her the way I had?

Finally I decided that if the right person came along, I would sell Unaweep. Four people came to look at her, but she didn't like any of them. She looked tense and scared, and she didn't like their pushiness. She depended on me to protect her, so I told them all no.

Then Linda arrived. I could see that Unaweep liked her and listened to her. Linda didn't scare her. Unaweep and I knew she was the one. And the parting wasn't so sad after all: I got to keep Unaweep in training at my barn.

LINDA'S STORY

I grew up reading books and playing the piano. My mother, although a wonderful woman, was overly protective of her children and didn't want us to get hurt. So, the normal scraped knees and broken arms from falling out of trees were not part of my childhood experience. As a result, I had confidence in my intellectual and musical abilities, but little confidence in my physical prowess.

When I was about eight, I rode my friend's Shetland pony in her pasture. Although I loved horses, it terrified me to go faster than a walk. But that love of riding never left me. In my twenties, I took some lessons that included jumping and trail riding. At age forty-six, I returned to horses again, taking week-long riding vacations in France or Wyoming. This meant building up my skill and confidence to ride up to eight hours a day or gallop five miles at a stretch.

At fifty-eight I finally bought my first horse, Abby, a beautiful six-year-old Paint. I knew little about owning a horse, and I didn't realize that Abby was still quite young and needed much more training. Nor were my goals clear: I wanted a horse and figured I would have her trained to do whatever I wanted her to do. Some months later I got interested in the idea of riding to music and then learned about freestyle reining. Combining them appealed to my musical and dramatic abilities—doing them on horseback seemed a dream come true. At the time I worked with a trainer who didn't believe in me or in my horse. She not only chipped away at my confidence, but also implied that I was too old and not good enough to compete.

To top it off, Abby wasn't built to be a reiner. I also found out she didn't have the personality for the job. I had a dream, but I couldn't achieve it with her. I refused to give up my dream, and I certainly wasn't going to sell my horse. Abby's new trainer encouraged me to buy a second horse and told me about one that lived five barns away. When I met Unaweep, I knew she was the one to help me fulfill my dream.

Since I'd lived a life of the mind, I had never been in tune with my body. With Unaweep, I realized that I was a better rider than I had thought, and my progress was swift. I grew more aware of what my body was doing: the position of my seat bones and my legs, the calmness of my hands, where my eyes focused, where my shoulder was. Unaweep was so well trained that she made learning the reining maneuvers fun. Much of my improvement came from the teaching of my new trainer, Danie, who assured me that my goals were not unrealistic with this horse. But a lot of it came from Unaweep's patience, her way of listening to me, and her responsiveness. I trusted her. She was protective of me and never went faster than she felt I could handle. I began to lose my fear.

But I wasn't sure if I could actually compete in freestyle reining. I decided to find out. For my sixtieth birthday, I planned a program set to music, riding both Abby and Unaweep. I rented an arena and performed in front of my friends. Through the experience I discovered a new kind of confidence and happiness.

Danie and I had both been confined by limitations: her "box" had been her bad first marriage, and mine had been my lack of confidence in my physical ability. Once we removed these negative influences and regained our confidence with the help of Unaweep, we both found fulfilling identities—Danie as a trainer and competitor and I as a horsewoman who has physical talent.

Three months after I bought Unaweep, Danie and both our husbands cheered me on as I competed in my first freestyle reining show in Rifle, Colorado. Most people enter reining competitions for years before trying freestyle, but I had come late to this game—I began with freestyle. I did my best and Unaweep was more responsive than she had ever been. To my great joy, we won third place, with extra points for artistry. That day, one dark sorrel mare carried two cowgirls closer to their dreams.

—Linda Seger and Danie Hewlett

In the Silence

Busy, busy, busy. That's all I've ever been. Not that there haven't been rewards. A satisfying career. Great kids. A husband who never minded my doing my own thing. In the beginning of our marriage, I playfully demanded one thing of him, "Never ask me to give up my horses. It would be very embarrassing to tell people your wife left you for a horse." He laughs at this memory today, but he never dared put it to a test over the years, even when we were short on money.

I've had horses in my life since I was seven years old. Most little girls grow out of this predictable phase, but I never did. I have always loved animals, but the bonds with my horses have been particularly strong. Curiously, horses became more important to me as I moved along in life, getting busier and busier with home, job, kids, husband, and all the other things that flash through a driven person's life. Driven to succeed in a career. Driven to be a good mom . . . good wife . . . keep a nice house. Always multitasking, making dinner with one hand stirring a pot, and concluding a work deal with the other hand clutching the phone.

Then an injury sparked an undetected immune disorder into a raging crisis. I had trouble doing the simplest of tasks. Thinking about dinner, stirring a pot, concentrating on work—all seemed too difficult. I could barely walk from the bed to a chair. A team of specialists concluded my disorder had no name yet. It was a mystery illness, somewhat like lupus but not lupus. Treatment regimens brought some improvement, but I have flare-ups from time to time. I wish that I could be normal again, but I accept that this disability is my new normal. The process of acceptance has been difficult. Who was I if I wasn't accomplishing several things at once?

While I pondered what my future held, my dear, sweet mother-in-law offered some wisdom, "You don't have to find the answer, let the answer find you." Nicky was deeply spiritual, and in her life journey she had learned how to be quiet and contemplative. We had grown very close over the course of twenty years. In many ways she was my mother, my wise woman, and my great, good girlfriend, but I was skeptical of her advice. I did not yet understand the value of silence or the feeling of trust that answers would come with patience.

When it became clear that I could no longer do full-time work, my husband encouraged me to quit my job and have fun with my horses. But just playing with horses seemed a little self-centered. I had a lot of time but little energy to do anything. Nicky reminded me often, "Learn how to be content with quietness. Trust the silence."

Suddenly the answer to my future arrived in the daily newspaper. A new organization in my community paired adult mentors with children in foster care. This group needed volunteers to commit ten hours a month for at least one year to be steady, caring, non-judging friends to children. The commitment would include outings in nature, the arts, meals together, and more. My five children were grown up, and I had truly enjoyed seeing them thrive. Perhaps I could help someone with a more difficult beginning in life to discover the possibilities.

Nicky was happy about my new direction and even happier that I had let it find me. I called her often to tell her of my adventures, which often included horses, with my new friend. My eight-year-old foster child had never been around horses before, but within a couple of months she was confidently helping me care for my quiet, well-mannered quarter horse, my big Thoroughbred-cross Paint, and my kid-safe Fjord pony. Now, after a year, my daughter laughingly says that, after trying so hard to spark the horse hobby in my own children, I finally have my horse-crazy little girl. All my children learned to ride, but none had the passion. This little girl in foster care has the passion. After a few months of lessons with me, I felt she was ready for her first horse show. The smile on her face as she came out of the arena with a first-place ribbon was one grand moment—for her and for me.

My husband's suggestion to "play with the horses" led me to not just accept but to treasure my new, less-active life. Something else was happening, too. The more time I spent with my horses, the better I felt. I didn't feel sick when I was riding out on the trail or mucking out a stall.

Just when I was settling into this new normal, Nicky was diagnosed with cancer that had already spread to her brain. She had only a few weeks to live. Family members and friends from all over traveled to her bedside to say a final "I love you." My sister-in-law, Libby, moved in with her and cared for her night and day until the end. We all did our best, but Libby was best of all, delivering care that was far better than any we could have paid for. I spent some time with Nicky when she still had energy and wanted to make plans. She took me by the hand and walked through the house pointing out things she wanted me to have after she was gone. "If you could name one thing you really, truly want, what would it be?" she asked.

"Do you have a St. Francis statue?"

"I should have guessed you would want the patron saint of animals in the garden. But I don't have one." She insisted we go shopping immediately.

"But I wanted it to come from your heart, not mine," I said.

"If you want it, then I want it for you. So it will in fact come from my heart when we find the right one." Nicky and I looked in several stores, but none of the St. Francis statues we found appealed to me. "We'll find an exquisite St. Francis." But we didn't. She died a few weeks later.

My husband wanted to do something to thank Libby for her extraordinary care of their dear mother. We wanted her to have a vacation, the trip of her dreams. I looked up five-star resorts and spas in California and gave Libby a list. I also included one very Spartan choice: a five-day silent retreat at a Camaldolese monastery on the Big Sur coast. In her work as a spiritual director who organizes and leads religious retreats, Libby has never been on a retreat as just a guest. The monks won hands down over the masseuses.

Libby flew in from Minneapolis, and I drove her down the rugged, winding coast road to the monastery. I had never been on a spiritual retreat myself. I don't think I had been completely silent a day in my life. But Nicky and Libby had told me that amazing things can happen when you spend some serious contemplative time in the right environment, so I decided to stay at the monastery for three days to see what it was all about. I was a little worried though. Wouldn't it require some profound thinking? I didn't know if I had the energy, talent, or intellect for such spiritual work. But I remembered Nicky's words about just letting things come to me, so I prepared myself to be quiet and receptive.

We arrived at the monastery after dark. A note on the door guided us to our rooms and asked us to register in the morning.

I awoke to the sound of bells as the monks signaled the call for morning worship. Outside the large windows of my room, I glimpsed heaven. I was perched on a hill overlooking the Pacific. Smooth blue water far below blended into a pastel sky as the sun peeked out from the hills behind my room. I went to check in at the bookstore, the one place on the grounds where talking was allowed. An angelic-looking woman behind the counter smiled. "Isn't this a glorious day! We've had nothing but gloomy fog for weeks on end." I thought, "How fitting to honor Libby's arrival." While the woman registered our names, I wandered around the bookshop. In one narrow corner, something made me stop and blink. It was a statue of St. Francis. Not just any statue, but an extraordinarily beautiful one. I ran my hand over his head and down his robe to the outstretched hands where birds and flowers perched. His expression was full of tenderness and love for all creatures. The statue was for sale, but it was expensive. I was trying to be careful with money so I walked away. I glanced back a couple of times as I left the shop for a morning walk down the spectacular, winding road to the ocean.

I tried to empty my mind and simply regard the beauty and silence. "Something is waiting for me. I need to listen." There were benches along the two-mile switchback to the main road below, and on the way back up I stopped to rest at each one. Every time I sat down, I thought about the statue in the bookstore. I was annoyed that I couldn't clear it from my thoughts. At the last bench, I took a deep breath and willed my mind to be as smooth and calm as the ocean below. There was that confounded statue again. All right, it won't go away, so what is it about this statue that has me transfixed? Everything. The statue's beauty. The expression on St. Francis's face. His hands, birds, flowers, bowl. St. Francis took care of God's creatures with food, love, and understanding. And then the tears came along with the message I had been waiting to receive. This was the St. Francis that Nicky meant for me—exquisite in every way. She had told me that when I found the right one, it would come from her heart.

I had worried this retreat would require hard work on my part because I would need to struggle to have profound thoughts. On that glorious first day, Nicky showed me what I had come to find: "Be quiet and trust the silence. Rewards will come." I bought the beautiful statue and placed it on the desk in my room overlooking the magnificent view. For the next two days, I gazed at St. Francis and thought about his tenderness for animals. I began to realize that my own love for my horses has come from their quietness. In all those years of being so busy, I never considered giving up my horses. Now I realized it wasn't just about horseback riding. It was about finding a quiet refuge in a speed-racing life. I had never really thought about the peace I always felt in their presence or the precise communication with them that requires no words. This was why I had advised my husband never to come between me and my horses—they were my sanctuary of quiet, my reward for honoring silence. I had known the feeling, but I couldn't have explained that in the frenzy that was my life all those years ago.

After vespers on my last night, Libby and I sat on a bench in silence to watch the sun set. Suddenly a beautiful fox walked toward us from the hill below. She seemed to want to join us on the bench. She approached to within inches of Libby's foot, looked at us, then retreated a few steps, only to repeat the effort several times. Finally, she ended her indecision and sat on a flat rock a few feet away. Still and quiet, she gazed at the sunset along with us. Libby and I glanced at one another in surprise and wonder. We were sharing a moment of grace. When the sky darkened, the fox disappeared down the hill. I'm sure my St. Francis was smiling.

At home, I placed St. Francis on the ridge that looks out at the snow-capped mountains. He watches over the barn where my horses are stabled. My cat stares longingly at the bowl he holds, hoping birds will stop there just long enough . . . but they don't. I look at St. Francis and think of Nicky, who taught me about silence. Much has come from being quiet, and all of it concerns healing. There is a precious, horse-crazy little girl who needed a chance to thrive, and an older, horse-crazy woman whose spirit needed renewing. The quiet world of the animals is helping us both find joy and healing in its silence.

—Sue Pearson Atkinson

Escape

The purple bruises stood out angrily on her arms as Ann clutched the steering wheel. But the bruises didn't hurt as much as the tongue-lashing she'd received that morning from her husband. "You're worthless. You have no friends," were the first of the nasty words he had snarled. Now she drove as quickly as she could toward the only relief she knew these days. She would go out of her mind if she couldn't find some peace for just a little while.

"No one likes you. Your whole family is crazy, and everyone knows it," her husband had said. Ann knew she would feel better as soon as she got to the barn and put her swollen face against her horse's warm body. "Your father's a drunk. Your mother's crazy. Your friends are using you." He had gone on and on. She could forget his hurtful words for a short time once she breathed in the comforting smell of her horse. "You're a terrible mother! The house is filthy! What do you do all day?" She tried to forget the morning and think instead about the ride she would take that day.

Her hands relaxed slightly on the wheel as she turned off the freeway. The landscape changed immediately. Now there were vast fields of soybeans on both sides of the road. Next year, the farmers would grow corn, and the year after that, beans again. Herds of horses in the distance reminded her that she would soon reach her destination. Once there, she could talk until her soul was purged of that morning's ugliness. Her horse would listen without judging; he had been her solace before and he would be her solace today.

Thinking of crop rotation reminded Ann of the cycle of life, how each generation nourished the next. She thought of her teenaged daughter, Nikki. Every day the mother planted seeds in the young mind. The seeds could be random acts of kindness, an appreciation for the beauty of nature, a love of horses. Ann believed it was her job to plant and nurture these seeds and hope they would flourish in her daughter. She imagined Nikki as one of the bean plants, reaching up to the sun and soaking up the rain, welcoming all that nature and the world had to offer, good or bad, with outstretched limbs, embracing life. Ann was proud of her daughter and felt that she was growing into a strong, sensitive woman.

The rich fields gave way to trees and wild forest, home to coyotes, squirrels, and red-tailed hawks. A stream twisted beside the road. Its steep banks sheltered foxes and an occasional otter. All these things seemed like a balm to Ann's red, swollen eyes. She saw them, and she relaxed even more. Soon she passed rolling hills patchworked with horse pastures and stitched together with split-rail fences. Bridle paths crossed the road, and she could see jumps in the distance. Horse country. As she passed a farm on the right, a stable on the left, Ann's lungs filled with the smells of hay, cut grass, and, best of all, horses.

She turned onto the gravel driveway between white board fences and drove beneath a canopy of pine trees. The trees brushed the top and sides of her car and caressed her mind. She took a left past the house, a right past the mossy green pond, and stopped at the barn.

Ann loved that barn. Long, low, and badly in need of paint, it felt homey and comfortable. She could truly relax here. There were two other boarders, but she was usually alone when she came out to ride in the afternoon. She could pretend the place was hers and clean the stalls, tidy up the tack room, polish tack, or make silly small talk to her horse without being embarrassed.

Jefferson heard the click of Ann's paddock boots on the cobblestones. He peered around the door of his stall and greeted her with his low, deep nicker. The very sound of it soothed Ann's soul. How could one little sound say so much? *I love you.*

I am happy to see you. Where's my treat? His muzzle reached out and sniffed her shirt and hands. She gave him a carrot and he chewed it noisily. Ann broke off little pieces of carrot and gave them to the other eight horses in the barn. She saved the last piece for Benny, an Australian shepherd dog that lived at the farm. Benny didn't really like carrots, but he ate his piece out of respect for Ann.

She regarded Jefferson. What a sight for sore eyes! The beauty of the seven-year-old bay Thoroughbred inspired her soul. At nearly seventeen hands, muscles rippled beneath his smooth coat, and intelligence glistened in his eyes. What did she do to deserve such a great horse? The truth of the matter was that she'd spent her life with horses, and she'd loved them all. They had probably all loved her in return, but right now, with her marriage on the rocks, Jefferson was her lifesaver. She already felt his healing powers work on her psyche. His warm breath blew over her face and calmed her mind. As she slowly stroked his smooth, brown neck, her own breathing slowed, too. Horses meant peace.

Ann threw him a flake of hay and got her brushes from the tack room. Then she curried the horse in his stall. Three years ago when she'd got him, she hadn't dared curry him in his stall—he was too restless. He would paw the ground so fiercely that his shoes dug holes in the floor. At that time, Jefferson was fresh off the racetrack. A leg injury retired him at four, and his personality made him a good candidate for rehabilitation and retraining as a riding horse. Little by little, he had calmed and mellowed. He trusted Ann now. Relaxed and quiet, he munched his hay as she brushed small circles on his back.

Jefferson had had the same effect on Ann. Countless were the times she had arrived at the barn in tears, trembling after an argument with her husband. She would place her shaking hands on the horse, lean her face into his side, and with closed eyes inhale his smell. That smell reminded her of her happiest childhood days. Breathing it in, she could escape her horrible marriage.

That morning's argument forgotten, Ann was now totally relaxed. She could hear the other horses turning in their stalls and eating. She could hear Benny softly panting at the stall door. Ann put the saddle and bridle on Jefferson and led him quietly from the barn.

The horse was as eager as Ann to get out on the trails. They skirted a swaying field of hay and crossed a creek. Jefferson tasted the water. Ann let him play in it a minute before urging him on. Once they reached the serene darkness of the wooded trail, they began to trot, and before Ann knew it they were cantering. Jefferson sailed eagerly over a coop jump. He was a terrific jumper, and Ann could keep up with him. Not bad for fifty-three, she thought.

Once, Ann and Jefferson had scared some deer. The deer leaped from the underbrush onto the trail, and for a few seconds horse and rider galloped in the center of the herd. Jefferson had looked around at his new friends and seemed to enjoy the chance to run with them. Ann felt she had glimpsed a piece of heaven. When the deer veered back into the woods, Jefferson wanted to follow them because, apparently, they loved to run as much as he did.

Ann exerted a steady pressure on the reins, guiding the Thoroughbred confidently. He trusted her now, but it hadn't always been that way. It had taken years for her to earn his trust. Those years had been full of positive rewards, not the least of which was their relationship. She felt blessed to own such a great horse.

Back at the barn she cleaned Jefferson carefully, put the tack away, and gave him a last carrot. Latching the rope across the aisle, she turned off the lights and walked to her car. She felt relaxed, young, and energized. She had run on long, slender legs and soared as light as a feather. She had been in perfect harmony with another living thing. For one afternoon at least, she had forgotten her abusive marriage, her age, her weight, her parents' failing health, and her daughter's less-than-stellar report card. As she settled in her car for the drive home, she remembered how her spirit had commingled with that of her strong, beautiful horse. Many times he had given her the gifts of love and trust, but today he had given her confidence. Now Jefferson's healing calmness stayed with her as Ann committed herself to the changes she would make.

—Nancy Alexander

Our Horse of Peace

My dream of owning a horse grew between the pages of *My Friend Flicka*. As I read for hours, I was transported onto Flicka's back, galloping free. Unfortunately, I lived in town and, as my dad pointed out every time I asked, a horse would not fit in the carport. Fortunately, I had many cousins who lived on farms and they had horses. I made a nuisance of myself during weekend visits until one cousin or another relented and took me riding. They didn't understand my obsession for grooming the horses; all they wanted to do was watch television.

When I grew up, summer jobs replaced the visits to the cousins. In college I decided to study social work. I liked to think it was because of my own experience in a foster home. Gratitude seemed to be the driving force behind my choice of career: perhaps I could give back some of what had been given to me over the years. The truth wasn't quite so altruistic. It happened to be the only major that didn't demand anything more rigorous than rudimentary math and science.

The state school I attended required its aspiring social workers to perform fifty hours of volunteer work. My foster parents thought this was a wonderful idea. Once I saw what I was getting myself into, they reasoned, I would come to my senses and become a dental hygienist like my cousin Sharon. But just as I knew that one day I'd have a horse, I also knew that I couldn't spend my days looking into people's mouths. In our church bulletin, I read that the Our Lady of Peace group home needed volunteers for its summer camp program. Activities included swimming, rafting, arts and crafts, and horseback riding. Here was divine intervention! I could finally have a horse—or at least use one—and still live in the city.

On my first day, I drove the short half-mile to Our Lady of Peace and parked in the staff lot. Dressed in jeans, T-shirt, and tennis shoes, with my riding boots stowed in the trunk of my car, I felt as luminous as the early summer sun. Soon I would be astride a soft, silky horse and showing others the joys of riding. Life could not get any better.

In the youth counselor's office I met David. "So where's the horse?" I smiled. "I'd like to get him ready for the kids." David rolled his eyes and sighed, just the way my cousins had, but he indulged me and took me through the convent-like building and out the back door to a dilapidated barn. One strong gust of wind and the whole structure would become firewood.

"We talked about selling Buttercup, but . . . ," David began, walking to the end of the barn. My first look at Buttercup was unreciprocated; his forelock had grown so thick and shaggy that his eyes were completely hidden.

"He can't see!" I said, pushing back the matted hair.

"Yeah, well, who's got time?" David shoved his hands into his pockets.

Undaunted, I rubbed Buttercup's silken nose. "I'll fix you up. You'll be good as new." I fed him some sugar cubes I'd brought from home.

"As long as we're out here let me show you the rest of the property," said David. "Group activities start at 10 A.M., so we have plenty of time." He walked out of the barn and back toward the main building. I looked at my watch and ran after him, trying to curb my excitement.

"Would you mind if I ran home and got some scissors? Buttercup can't be ridden like he is, and I want the kids to enjoy him." David sighed the same way my foster parents had every time I'd begged for a horse, but he finally nodded, something Dad never did. "It will only take fifteen minutes. I live so close I could walk," I said as I ran toward the parking lot.

Soon I was back, armed with my mother's dressmaking shears. I marched to the barn and fed Buttercup a carrot. His hair wasn't the only thing that needed improvement; his belly was so large I didn't think a girth would fit around it. "You'll feel better once you can see," I told him. Visions of Flicka ran through my head. All Buttercup needed was a good grooming. I picked up his forelock, positioned the scissors, and squeezed. Nothing. His hair was too thick. I separated out a strand and cut it to reveal a large brown eye staring at me. "Hi, Buttercup," I said, immensely pleased.

Bit by bit, I cut through his forelock and mane. Periodically, I stepped back to assess my handiwork and admire Buttercup's old but handsome face as it emerged from behind its shroud.

"How's it going?" David approached with a group of girls and boys.

"Great!" I said, anxious to make a good impression on the kids.

"Is he supposed to look like that?" asked a girl of about eleven.

"I'm just getting started," I explained as I tried to even out the chunky forelock, which was getting shorter and shorter but no straighter.

"He looks like my little sister when she cuts her own hair," declared a freckle-faced boy.

"I'm sure once she's finished Buttercup will be good as new. Who wants to play kickball?" David asked, drawing the group outside. I gave Buttercup one final snip before joining them. "I'll fix you later," I promised.

Horseback riding fell on Tuesday and Thursday mornings. For two hours, I had four kids and Buttercup to myself. On those days I arrived well before the scheduled start time of

9:30 to give Buttercup his oats and fresh water. He had been neglected for so long, I felt he needed more attention than just the scheduled four hours a week. The extra time I spent grooming and walking him produced side benefits: soon I could cinch his saddle girth tight.

On that first Tuesday when I stood in the shade of the barn and watched my four would-be riders run toward me, my heart felt their excitement. They stood in a semicircle around me, and I smiled into their upturned faces. "Are you ready to learn?" I asked. I was certain that they were as eager to soak up whatever horse knowledge I could impart as I was to share it.

"I thought we were gonna ride?" asked Steven, the freckle-faced boy.

"We will. But riding a horse isn't that simple. Buttercup needs our help first." I led them into the cool, damp shadow of Buttercup's stall.

"Why's he tied like that?" Allison asked. She had pulled her long brown hair into a ponytail that fell in thick waves down her back, just the way I imagined Buttercup's tail would look with a lot of TLC.

"Before anyone can ride him his hooves have to be picked clean of any stones or he could go lame," I said as I checked the ropes that held Buttercup's head in place. Running my hand down his rear flank, I lifted a hoof and showed the kids how to clean it.

"I'm not doin' that. He'll step on me," said Steven as he backed up to sit on a hay bale. The other three quickly joined him.

"You don't have to. I just want you to understand what's involved in taking care of a horse."

"We thought we were gonna ride," Elizabeth wailed as she sucked on a chunk of her hair.

Releasing Buttercup's leg, I stood up. "I'm glad you're all so excited to ride. Buttercup is wonderfully gentle, but he's a living creature and needs our time and attention if we want something from him." I studied each face, searching for a glimmer of understanding. Steven pulled at a straw in the hay bale; Elizabeth chewed her hair; Allison bit her thumbnail; and John looked at the ground. Not a good start.

"Okay, one more thing, and then we'll take turns riding," I said and watched all four pairs of eyes dance with joy. "You know . . . ," I began, and planted my hands on my hips. It made me sound and feel like my foster mom when she was about to lecture me. I started over.

"Who likes dessert?" Four hands shot up high. "Imagine Buttercup is dessert." All four heads nodded and hungry looks replaced the vacant stares. "Before you can have dessert, you have to eat the meal. But before you eat the meal, what happens?"

"Somebody makes it!" Elizabeth shouted, spitting out her hair.

"Exactly. And before that, what happens? Where does the cook get the food?"

"The store! You have to buy groceries," Steven yelled.

"Right. And before that?"

"A farmer grows it?" Allison whispered.

"That's right. So what does this have to do with our delicious dessert of Buttercup?" I asked. The three looked at John, who had not spoken at all. His gaze focused on his torn tennis shoes as they kicked up a small cloud of dirt. "Anyone?" I asked, not wanting to make John feel uncomfortable.

"We have to fix everything before he's ready to eat," said John, turning red. The other kids howled with laughter at his mistake. "John's gonna eat a horse!" they cried in sing-song unison.

"That's right!" I shouted over the top of their noise. "We're all going to eat a horse. We're going to enjoy everything Buttercup can give us. And John gets to go first." I quickly saddled Buttercup and put the bit in his mouth. Then I helped John swing his stocky leg up and over and led boy and horse out into the summer sun. The other three jumped and skipped behind us, anxious for their turns.

Buttercup time on Tuesday and Thursday took on a rhythm of its own. Taking care of a horse was more difficult than I had ever imagined. It required time, patience, and diligence. It occurred to me that it was not unlike teaching the kids at Our Lady of Peace how to cope with the challenges in their young lives. By focusing on a horse, the kids learned a little about the ebb and flow of healthy, caring relationships.

I know I learned much more from the kids and Buttercup. When I arrived, I just wanted a chance to ride and pretend I had a horse of my own. I left with an unshakable certainty that I wanted to be a social worker. I knew then that I could bring a little peace into the tumultuous lives of foster children.

—Sharla Rae Jahnke

photography ©IStockphoto.com/Jean-Yves Beredeyt

The Promise

In memory of David Patrick Moynihan

When David called me on that Sunday afternoon,
he was well past his fortieth birthday and once
again rising above the demons of his addiction.
He'd had a rough time at The Ranch, an extended-
care treatment facility for addiction and trauma

recovery where I work as the equine psychotherapist, but ultimately it had been productive for him. We watched him emerge from a life ruled by fear into a place of comfort and autonomy that he had never before experienced. His relationship with a leggy, sixteen-hand palomino quarter horse helped his transformation. Badger may well have been the best therapist David ever met.

Like David, Badger's life before The Ranch had not been easy. Badger was the real deal: an honest-to-goodness, working ranch horse. Through seven hot summers and bitterly cold winters, he had carried cowboys and worked cattle. By the time he showed up in my equine therapy program, he was, to put it mildly, not the cuddliest animal I'd ever seen. He was anxious about being handled roughly. Even simple grooming annoyed him, unless it was done with gentle fingers and soft brushes.

The good news for both Badger and David was that they came to understand each other at a deep and spiritual level. Badger's head would rest against David's chest while David brushed his relaxed golden neck. These two souls found a way around the stereotypes of masculine toughness to connect as friends in a sacred emotional space. There is nothing more healing than that.

David spent more than two months at The Ranch. He dove into his work. At first, he needed lots of support in my equine groups; later, as he gained confidence, he was the one teaching and demonstrating the equine concepts to new residents. He found a place where he could be himself. His mother later told me that even though David knew his family loved him, he had never felt understood by anyone until he came to The Ranch.

Truthfully, we just provided a place where he could finally begin to honor himself.

After leaving The Ranch, David continued to struggle with his recovery, but he held on to enough of what he had learned to reach out for help when he needed it. One day he called and asked for a reunion with Badger. He had hit some rough spots, but he wanted to get past them. As I listened to him, I envisioned a fist raised in determination. David hadn't given up. And he was reaching out to the life force he had connected with the year before.

"I want to get back up on Badger," he told me. Of course, I agreed. We ended the call with plans to talk again soon to set a date.

Two days later, David was killed in a car accident. Those who loved him were crushed—his mom and dad, two brothers and their wives, four nieces, and two nephews. The death of such a young man is always tragic, but there was something especially heartbreaking about David's death at a time when hope was re-entering his life.

The Ranch is a very special place, where much more than psychotherapy happens. Even though we believe in the traditional tenets of mental health treatment, we believe even more in the goodness and truth of our residents, in their right to choose how they live their lives, and in their ability (and responsibility) to create their own reality. Recovery is an adventure and a privilege. David, a man without a malicious bone in his body, had found his way into our hearts. We decided to gather in memory of him. We invited his family to join us for a "circle of remembering."

On the appointed day, David's parents, as well as one of his brothers and sister-in-law, gathered in a circle in the garden. Some of us offered gifts or flowers along with some final words. I laid a few strands of Badger's mane and tail among the flowers and said that this was my way of keeping my promise to reunite David and Badger. We all cried. At the end of the ceremony his mother came to me with tears in her eyes and asked, "Could I have some of the horse's mane?"

"Sure you can," I said. "Would you like to meet Badger?"

From her grief-filled face there came a light into her eyes. "Can we?"

I took them to the barn and went to retrieve Badger. I can't explain what happened next. Badger isn't the most affectionate or friendly horse; at times, he's just plain grouchy. David had been one of the select few who had been able to find the horse's hidden tenderness. As Badger and I walked from the pasture, I tried to communicate to him my hope that he would be nice to our visitors. David's parents—no longer young—hung on the pasture gate like eager children waiting for a riding lesson. As we neared, his mother hesitantly reached her fingertips to touch the palomino's powerful neck.

There was so much need in this simple action that I told her that she could come closer. The tiny woman stepped up to the big horse, stroked his neck, and greeted her son's friend, "David sure did love you." She was standing in the same place her son had stood, loving the same horse, and I imagined that she was aware of this, too.

"It's okay to hug him if you want," I smiled.

Another step closer and slowly her arms wrapped around Badger's neck and quietly held him. I touched Badger's nose. "Thank you," I thought.

Personal recovery work can be sacred. Much of David's work at The Ranch certainly had been, and so was this quiet, unexpected moment. The rest of the family stepped up to touch Badger. David's brother asked if he could take some of the mane to his children.

I've been a therapist for twenty years, but what I experienced that day was unique and profound. Still emotional as I drove home that evening, it became clear that I needed to find the words to describe this powerful experience and express its importance. Later, as I talked with my husband about the day, I understood what I had witnessed. David's mother, with her arms wrapped around Badger's neck, had given her son the final hug, an embrace she hadn't been able to give. With the help of a big, palomino ranch horse, a grieving mother said goodbye to her son.

—Dede Beasley, M.Ed., L.P.C.

My Therapist

My normal workday begins early, so I rise when my radio clicks on and WJJZ's smooth jazz starts to waft across my bedroom at 4:30 A.M. Today I can't decide what exercise regimen to do. I ponder my choices: a seven o'clock yoga class would ease my arthritis, but it would mean working an hour later in my windowless basement office to make up for class time; an afternoon at the gym would do my cardiovascular system good; a hike on the cross-country trails through the changing fall colors sounds appealing. I hear on the radio that today will be sunny and warm. That settles it. There's no way I'm staying past two-thirty or working out in a gym if it's going to be that nice outside. I decide that a horseback ride would be the perfect exercise for today. I pack my lunch, swallow a quick breakfast, glance at the morning newspaper, and head off to work.

Usually I spend my workday making office visits to university staff and faculty with computer problems. But today is my designated "trouble ticket day," the one day each week when I'm required to be at my desk. Any staff person, faculty member, or student who is having computer problems can call the desktop support unit. Today that support unit is me. If possible, I troubleshoot the problem over the phone. If the problem is more serious, I schedule an office visit.

By day's end I'm frustrated, exhausted, and in desperate need of some sunshine. I look out the loading-dock door. The sun is nowhere in sight. A chilly wind swirls the fallen leaves on the pavement, and the temperature is a damp fifty-six degrees. "So much for sunny and seventy," I mutter at the dreary sky as I grab my tote bag and head out the door. I've already decided that I'm going riding even if it isn't warm or sunny.

Virgil is my friend Mary Jean's flea-bitten gray Thoroughbred. He's twenty-three but acts like a teenager. Standing just shy of sixteen hands high, he has a big head, alert ears, and kind eyes. He sports a gorgeous platinum mane and tail and has a heart as big as Texas. Virgil has been a racehorse, a pony clubber, and a three-day eventer. He can be quite intimidating to the uninitiated. Although semi-retired now, Virgil still enjoys a cross-country hack, a paper chase, or a fox hunt.

When I go to fetch him from his pasture, Virgil raises his head high like a giraffe. Ears forward, eyes alert, he watches my approach. Unrestrained and feeling playful, he spins, rears for a quick spar with his pasture partner, does a drop kick, and gallops off with a catch-me-if-you-can attitude. He's fast. His feet are like springs, and his back bounces like a trampoline as he turns and prances toward me, snorting with excitement. I stand my ground. He halts inches away. Gently, he nuzzles my hand for a carrot and stands still for his halter.

If Virgil spots the truck and horse trailer parked in the driveway, he knows that we're going for a hack in the country and instantly becomes difficult to handle. Today there is no trailer in the driveway, so Virgil falls asleep in the cross-ties. That's fine with me. After a tough day at work, I don't need more aggravation. I curry and brush him, comb his mane, pick out his feet, and put on his saddle. I rouse Virgil from his daydreams to put on his bridle, then coax him down to the arena.

Virgil is like Dr. Jekyll and Mr. Hyde: when he's feeling good and happy, he transforms himself from a sleepy old nag into a high-level dressage showman. Today his warm-up walk and trot are fluid and free. His powerful neck stretches down, and his back muscles lift as his haunches begin to swing from side to side with every overstepping stride. He reaches for the connection between the bit and my hands.

We trot in twenty-meter circles interspersed with up-and-down transitions and direction changes. Virgil is engaged with me from his head to his tail. His ears swivel back and forth as his listens to my voice. He sensitively reacts to my position on his back. I lean back, and he slows. I stop my seat, and he stops. I sit deep in the saddle, pushing with my seat, and he gives me forward momentum. He responds to my slightest leg pressure, bending around it, moving away from it, or being energized by it. I request a turn on the forehand, and his haunches swing around in a 180-degree circle, while his front legs remain nearly motionless. His halts are square and prompt, his contact light and responsive. We are partners in the human-equestrian dance known as dressage.

I float on air as Virgil extends his trot across the diagonal, flicking each hoof forward in momentary suspension before reconnecting with the rapidly passing ground. We glide, shoulder-in, down the long side. We halt. Virgil stands in absolute submission. I ask, and he springs from a standstill into a rhythmic canter. My lower back relaxes and follows the collected rhythm of his rocking-chair motion. Oh, that I could possess such control in my workaday life!

Sir Winston Churchill once said, "There is something about the outside of a horse that is good for the inside of a man." If he'd lived at a different time, he would have included women.

Virgil is my salvation and my therapist; he listens to me and rejuvenates me. At the end of one more workday, my frustrations evaporate. The wind caresses my face as the crisp fall air fills my lungs and refreshes my brain. I am ready for whatever tomorrow may bring.

—Judi A. Brown

Trail Mix

It was in Los Angeles that I bought my first horse, Moonshadow. The sixteen-hand, blue-roan quarter horse was described to me by his former owner as a good "packer," or trail horse, and for several months, it was nothing but bliss between us.

Then, on a typical Saturday full of errands and housework, tragedy struck. I was fatigued from working all week, but Moonshadow needed to be ridden. By the time my chores were done and he was saddled it was 6 P.M. The sun would set around seven, leaving time for an hour's ride.

I was eager to take Moonshadow new places. After we successfully completed several exercises on the nearby mountain trails, we made our way along the path by the creek. The sounds of wildlife began to intensify, and Moonshadow started to get spooky and struggle against the reins. I could feel his resistance build beneath me, but I pressed on.

Suddenly a flock of starlings burst out of the reeds, their dark wings thrashing the air around our heads. Moonshadow bolted. Black mane flying, he zigzagged along the edge of the creek. I fell off and landed on my hands and knees with a loud, sickening crack.

I tried to get up—I wanted to be like those cowboys in the movies who recover immediately from any mishap—but my left leg wouldn't move at all, my right knee had ballooned to three times its normal size, and my left forearm dangled in a V. Moonshadow was gone. I swore I would sell him.

Night settled around me. The full moon lit the tall, dry grass where I lay, the surrounding sycamore trees, and the craggy peaks of the mountains. The park came alive with chirping and croaking, hooting and howling. Crickets. Frogs. Owls. Coyotes. And some startling noises I couldn't identify. I grabbed a nearby stick with my one good arm. If a coyote or cougar came near, I was going to put up one helluva fight. But mostly I was just going to lie still, listen, and wait. "*Someone* will come for me," I repeated like a mantra.

Hours ticked by, and I shivered uncontrollably. Shock protected me from the excruciating pain I should have been feeling. Instead, I felt as though I'd overdosed on coffee. Every fifteen minutes I checked my watch. Where was Moonshadow?

Finally I heard the clip-clop of hooves and someone calling my name. I saw the beam of a flashlight scanning the ground. It was my neighbor, Frank, riding Moonshadow. When he spotted me, he rode down the embankment.

"Frank, I'm hurt real bad," I choked back a sob. It was the first time I had admitted it to myself.

"Don't worry, doll," he said. "Everything's going to be okay. I've already called 911."

In the emergency room, the doctors kept me laughing while they poked and probed, and when the x-rays were over, they told me that besides breaking my arm, I had shattered both legs so badly they needed to be pinned together. My life would never be the same.

A week after surgery, I was transferred to a hospital that specialized in trauma rehabilitation, where I stayed for six weeks, undergoing more surgery and a blood transfusion. I gasped the first time I saw the x-rays of the pins in my legs. They weren't the little straight pins I'd imagined; they looked more like a mechanic's tools—big titanium screws and rods that made me look like a robot. I wanted my old body and my old life back so badly that I couldn't stop crying. Finally, they sent in a psychiatrist, who asked if I thought my horse felt guilty.

Two months later, I returned home in a wheelchair. It was impossible for me to get to Moonshadow's corral. Sometimes I could see his profile from my bedroom window. I had to cover my ears when I heard other horses clopping down the street with their riders. I wished that I had died that night in the park.

My first reunion with Moonshadow came on a cold winter's night when my friend Diane bundled me up and pushed my wheelchair down the steep driveway and over the rocky ground to his corral. He came to the railing and stared down at me. From my seat, Moonshadow looked huge. His new winter coat was thick and furry; his breath shot out of his nostrils in short white puffs. He terrified me.

Our next meeting came a month later when I was learning how to use a walker. At first I had to set little goals for myself, such as walking from my bed to the window—an accomplishment that left me breathless. So it was a big day when I walked from the end of my driveway over to the corral. My steps were slow and small. Walking on uneven ground required leg muscles that I hadn't yet redeveloped. When I finally made it, I clung to the bars and stood nose-to-nose with Moonshadow. We breathed into each other's nostrils. His coat smelled like sweet alfalfa. I stroked his long, shaggy mane.

For two months I was overly cautious around him, well aware of what his strength and size could do to me. One time when I leaned on the corral bars, Moonshadow picked up my nearby walker with the tip of his nose and threw it aside like a person would toss a pillow on a couch. "That thing is my legs!" I thought as I clung to the fence to retrieve it. But little by little I became comfortable again in his company. The first time I went inside his corral—seven months after the accident and walking with a cane—I longed to climb on his back.

Even after all I'd been through, there was no question in my mind about wanting to ride again. To me, it seemed as obvious a next step as walking unassisted. But would I be able to ride? One surgeon said that physically I should be capable, but mentally could be another story. Another surgeon asked, "Aren't you a little old to still be crazy about horses?" But the best advice came from my internist, who said that if riding was what I felt passionate about, then I should do it. Most people never find their passion. I knew I *needed* to ride. Then my friend Sandi had an idea: I should enroll in a program that teaches disabled people how to ride.

So, one Saturday I arrived at Special Equestrian Riding Therapy. Nora, the caring, no-nonsense program director, knew when to push her students beyond what they thought they could do. She quickly assessed my physical condition and led me to a high mounting platform where a small, gray Arabian mare named Kaffeyn waited.

I panicked. "*Caffeine?* I'm not getting on this horse!"

Nora assured me that the twenty-six-year-old mare's galloping days were over. I sat down on her woolen bareback pad like I would sit in a chair and slowly swung my leg over her neck. We set off with a person walking on each side and another guiding the mare with a lead rope. I clung to the pad, terrified of falling off. My fractured hip screamed, "I can't take this kind of movement!" When I was finally standing on the ground again, Nora gave me a hug, and I burst into tears.

The next Saturday I went back, and the Saturday after that. I stayed with the program for one year. My disability seemed minor compared to those of my classmates. I watched their progress and achievements despite Down syndrome, cerebral palsy, or deformed feet from an abusive childhood. We all worked hard to overcome our impairments, and every Saturday we applauded each other. When I felt comfortable riding many different horses and could canter again, I knew it was time to leave the group and ride Moonshadow.

Although I vowed we would never go on another trail ride alone, I was still nervous on his back, which made him nervous. I could see that glint of stubbornness in his eyes. I tried awfully hard to make it work—only riding him at a walk and only with other riders—but I always got a queasy feeling in my stomach, expecting him to bolt. The only thing for me to do was give him up and it made me feel like a failure.

My friend Diane came through for me and found him a good home with a more confident rider. He was a perfect gentleman when the young woman came to try him out, and I sadly watched her load him into her trailer. It was the final blow after divorce ended my marriage, and I was forced to sell my dream house.

For months I didn't know if I would ever own another horse. But then at a party I met a friend of a friend, and the next thing I knew I owned a small Arabian mare. Mollie has known the pain of an accident, too. Her left eye was lacerated by a piece of metal roof in a windstorm. She has adjusted to her prosthetic eye, just as I have adjusted to my artificial hip. We make a good pair: she has strong legs, and I provide the eyesight on her left side. She is calm and sweet, and I can feel my confidence returning.

Recently, I decided to take Mollie on a trail ride. As I saddled her up, I felt the butterflies twirling in my stomach. I talked to her in an effort to calm myself. After I tightened the girth, I got on her back, and we headed out.

My dog ran ahead and flushed wild rabbits and quail out of the cacti, scrub oak, sage, and mustard that border the sandy trails. As we neared the river, Mollie pricked up her ears at the shouts and laughter of people playing in the water. My body tensed. I focused on the space between her ears and said quietly to myself, "Sit back in the saddle and breathe deep." Mollie knew I was nervous, so I added, "I am a confident rider." Out of the corner of my eye, I saw a hummingbird land on a twig. The tiny bird on the thin branch teetered in the wind. I tried not to think about the fragility of my bones.

Halfway around the trail, we came upon a stand of syca-more trees and a white wooden cross with some plastic flowers stuck in the ground. I read the words on the cross: *In memory of Lynn F. Bush, November 3, 1949 – December 25, 2002.* The poor woman died on Christmas Day. What happened to her? Did she die on the trail? Had she been horseback riding? These thoughts made me anxious, so I moved on.

We were almost to the big rocks near the willows at the end of the trail. Mollie could see the ranch, and she picked up her pace. I told her what a good girl she was. We passed between the two boulders and started to cross the little bridge. On my right was a jagged-edged fence and on the other side of the fence, a ravine. On my left, cars came down the street toward the ranch. Mollie was excited and in a hurry. I pictured her rearing up and pitching me onto the fence, but Mollie was completely focused. As soon as I dismounted back at the ranch, I gave her a big hug.

Eleven years after my accident on the trail with Moonshadow, Mollie and I went on a trail ride together—alone.

—Wendy Beth Baker

Choosing to Lose

When I first met BJ, he was broken. Not broken in, just broken. A shattered soul. With a knife-edge back, thin neck, and torn hide, he looked like the poster horse for an animal rescue society. In his short career as a racehorse, he had finished last in three races. After he failed at his last start, he was turned out in a back paddock where he waited for the slaughterhouse. For two years he languished, unfed, uncared for, unloved, and unwanted, through the blistering heat of summer and the hail and sleet of winter. Forgotten.

Until I found him.

BJ was everything I didn't want in a horse. His lice-ridden, shaggy winter coat couldn't hide the staring ribs; his mane and tail were thick with burrs and tangles. I cringed when he moved into the stable next to my sleek, gray eventer, Hobbs. What communicable diseases did BJ have? How soon could I get him scrubbed up and respectable enough to sell? He was so weak when I first rode him that he lasted only ten minutes before he lay down in the arena, unable to go on. Every day I wondered what I had gotten myself into.

One day BJ caprioled in the lunge ring, fell, and smashed the stifle of his hind leg. For months he couldn't move. He could only stand in his yard, depressed, with his head hanging down. Useless, he was relegated to a back paddock—again.

Only this time he wasn't forgotten. He had a rug and food. And he had me. Every day I fed him. Because he couldn't move, I handed him wisps of hay and handfuls of grain.

One day when I tried to pat him, he backed away—limped, really. Not far, just enough to touch the electric fence. One zap and he decided that backing away wasn't the smartest move. With nowhere else to go, his only choice was to reach out, snuffling. The touch of his soft velvet nose was like a lover's caress. His lips fluttered over my flat-palmed hand, whiskers tickling, so respectful he might have deposited a sigh upon my outstretched fingers, or a kiss.

This wasn't the predatory approach of Hobbs, with his grasping teeth—too bad if your fingers got in the way—flattened ears and swishing tail, angry Rambo eyes and attitude. No, this was Gregory Peck, all caring and polite, the sensitive New Age gelding with the "woe is me" doleful eyes. As BJ begged for love, head resting on my shoulder, I lost myself to him.

His body and spirit healed with time. When he was strong enough to gallop, I discovered the reason for his dismal racing career. If he led, he slammed on the brakes so the horse he was running with could pass him. If he trailed, he ran as fast as he had to in order to stay on the heels of the leader, but he never passed it. No whip or spur could make him.

He chose to lose.

Choosing to lose, for a racehorse, earns the death penalty. But fate had stepped in and given him back his life and hope.

We shared ten years of glory and winning, broken bones and dreams, mist-shrouded nights and frost-clad mornings. Eventing, show jumping, dressage, and sidesaddle, he excelled at them all. But despite the trophies and ribbons of blue, his greatest gift was standing still, wrapped in night's raiment. While pale stars drifted in the ebony sky, he listened to my dreams and my failures, my secrets and my tears. He was a silent confidant without rebuke, scorn, or chastisement. He offered unconditional acceptance and love, his patient ears flicking back and forth as he let my voice float in and out and calmly accepted my outpourings of love or grief.

But then it came my turn to face purgatory. I succumbed to the blackest depths of despair cloaked in the innocuous term of "depression"—an illness to some, a curse to others, misunderstood by many. Of the causes, there were too many to name; some of them insidious. A cruel word here, a cutting remark there, lies and deceit, over time they added up to workplace harassment.

Sticks and stones may break my bones, but words can never harm me. Well, yes, they can. I know because I've been on the killing end of words sharper than a rapier, more lethal than a dagger stuck into your back. Spoken or written, they can be enemies, and they can haunt you for eternity.

The cruelty of one human to another knows no bounds. In the space of a year, cruel words obliterated joy, extinguished my self-confidence, and destroyed my life. I could have stood screaming with pain in a room full of people, but only BJ saw the hurt, the desperation, the loneliness, and the fear. I was always crying, but nobody understood. Only BJ heard the sobbing and felt his mane soaked with tears as I buried my face in his neck, breathing in the warm, comforting smell of horse. Only BJ knew of the darkness that was deeper than black because, in his own way, he had been there.

Who would put me back together when I broke? Who would stop my backing away from the hand of friendship? Who would save me?

I already knew the answer. It was staring at me with two limpid brown eyes. *Can't you see?* he seemed to be saying. *I'll save you. Who else listens while you cry? Who else stands by you when the knife hovers over your wrist? Whose neigh is it that calls you back from that dark place inside you?* BJ stamped an angry white-socked hoof. *You are responsible for me. What will happen to me if you go away? You saved me once. Don't send me back to that life of despair. Slit my throat first. Let my lifeblood course down your arms. When my legs buckle and I sink to the snow grass beneath the sweet-scented winter wattle, catch my falling head and ease it down. Caress me with the gentleness of the whispering wind while my eyes grow blank. Or let me save you. The choice is yours.*

Yes, the choice was mine: to fight a battle through the courts, live in misery while evading more daggers in the back, and win, or to walk out, regain my life, and lose.

I used to believe that winning was everything. I was told at every turn, "Fight the bastards. Don't let them win." But there are some battles that cannot be fought, some wars that cannot be won. Like BJ, I'd been worn down. I couldn't have moved one more step down that path without my knees buckling. I had neither the strength, the will, nor, indeed, the courage. I wanted a knight in shining armor to come and rescue me. I didn't realize that my knight was already there—in a coat made of hair instead of iron, with four legs, not two. His wordless comfort met my wordless pain. His strong Thoroughbred heart helped to heal my broken one.

I chose to lose. I slammed the door on a dark place that was hell on earth. It took some sort of courage to throw away a career of fifteen years and face the great unknown. It took courage to start again. Maybe I wasn't a coward after all.

Time to gallop, jump, fly. Time to lean low over a neck stretched out, black mane streaming on the wind, hooves beating out their wild music, the heart of the world beating through golden everlastings. Time to sway with the rhythm and enjoy the superb sensation of flight without wings.

I have since found a workplace where kindness rules the heart and fairness the mind. And BJ has found his place in another back paddock where he is neither alone nor forgotten, where he is lord over fifteen companions, none of whom mind him trailing at their heels.

BJ showed me that it's not about the races we win, it's how we choose to run the race, to take risks, to abandon everything we thought was true. I gave him everything when he had nothing. He gave me a reason to survive in my darkest time. BJ showed me that sometimes, just sometimes, when we choose to lose, we win.

—Linda Karen Dicmanis

The Strength to Return

I stood at the paddock fence and sobbed. It was still summer, and horses grazed in the pastures around me. Their necks arched gracefully down as they moved through the pasture seeking fresh grass. At the barn, a large bay mare leaned her head out her door, stared at me, and then returned to her hay. I kept crying, gulping now and then through the tears.

The woman standing there looked uncomfortable. She was in her fifties, wearing sagging, dirt-covered sweats, a manure rake propped up against the full wheelbarrow behind her. She'd never met me before and yet here I was, a thirty-year-old stranger bawling in front of her. "I'm sorry, honey," she said softly, "but I just can't give you riding lessons unless you have health insurance."

I pretended that I was fine although I was anything but. I didn't know it at the time, but I was in the middle of a major depressive episode, one that amplified life's simple challenges into tragedies.

I'd gone to the barn that day seeking comfort. Earlier that morning, I'd been deeply hurt by a friend at church. She had verbally attacked me, knocking me breathless with her anger. As she stormed out of the room in front of our friends and community, I'd stared, shocked and shaken, terrified that she would return and lash out at me again. Afterwards, I drove straight to a boarding stable I had heard about. I felt small and vulnerable, and I knew what I needed: a thousand pounds of power and compassion. A horse.

But the closest I came to a horse was the fence. Horses ambled toward me, and I offered them my open hand as I'd been taught to do as a child. Their noses were soft, their breath felt warm on my skin. Even though I was caught in the dark wave of depression and felt as though I would crumple into nonexistence at any moment, I started to feel myself come alive. Just the tickle of a horse's whiskers on my hands awakened something in me.

Feeling timid, I had approached the only person I saw, the owner of the boarding stable. I had asked her the question that would trigger the embarrassment of crying, the same question I had asked my parents years before: "Can I take riding lessons?" And even though I was no longer ten years old, the answer was still neither yes nor no.

I walked away from the barn, away from the horses, trying not to smell the most wonderful scent that has ever touched girl-kind, the earthy, salty scent of horses. I was crying, but I could still smell their scent on my hands. I carried that scent home.

Later that week, I was diagnosed with both depression and anemia. Awakened to life by my brush with the horses, I became proactive about my health care. I found health insurance for myself and for my husband. I researched therapeutic options and medications. With my doctor's blessing and guidance at each step, I made my own choices. I began to take iron supplements and antidepressant medication.

For the next month I lay exhausted on the couch. My muscles felt old and heavy, as if weighted down with rocks. "Perfectly normal when starting antidepressants," my doctor said. Lying there with barely enough energy to keep my eyelids open, I did not feel normal. But I tried to remember that my idea of "normal" had been skewed for years by depression.

Throughout this ordeal, my husband, a man with the build and gentleness of a draft horse, supported me, uplifted me, and quietly urged me to return to the barn.

"But I barely have the strength to walk to the refrigerator," I said. Rather than argue, he simply brought the contents of the fridge to me. He took care of all of my needs, took care of our home and animals, and simply allowed me to heal. When I didn't believe it myself, he truly believed that I would get better.

And I did. As my energy slowly increased, I began to notice the fascinating details of our world—the sun slanting across the surface of water, the thrust in my calves as I walked through the sand, the soft touch of my husband's hands, the look of a genuine smile. In these moments of discovery, I noticed one detail again and again—I couldn't seem to escape it—the phone number of the boarding stable amid the jumble of papers on my refrigerator. Sure, I felt good again, better than I had felt in years. But doubts nagged me. I didn't believe that feeling good could last.

Nonetheless, I made the call. I spoke again with the stable owner, told her that I now had health insurance, and got ready to beg. But begging wasn't necessary; she agreed right away. We made an appointment.

The day before I was scheduled to ride, I became wracked with nerves. On the day of my lesson, I forgot to arrive. I called the barn in a panic, apologized, and scheduled another lesson. This time I *had* to go, no matter how much I doubted myself— after sobbing at the stable owner at the paddock fence and then standing her up for my first lesson, I had to save face. I arrived at the stable for my second appointment wearing stretch pants, sweater, and thrift-store boots. I blinked when I saw a beautiful chestnut gelding cross-tied outdoors.

"This is Max," said the owner, now my teacher, patting her horse and looking at him with soft eyes. He was huge. His coat gleamed red and gold. Max glanced at me as I stroked his neck, back, and mane. His flesh felt warm beneath my hands. He smelled like hay and dust and sunshine. He felt quiet, not just outwardly, but inwardly, as though he trusted my teacher so much that he could fall asleep and know she would take care of him.

My teacher taught me the basics of horse safety. I was to stay close to Max, always touching him, always in contact, letting him know where I was so that if he kicked I could push back. (By then I was so taken with Max that I wanted to be in contact with him always.) I was to feed Max with my hand open and flat so that my fingers never came near his teeth. (By then I was so in love with Max that I wanted to hand feed him mints all day, just to feel his muzzle on my palm.)

And then I got to ride. Raised sixteen hands above the ground, I felt at once terrified and on top of the world. By the end of my lesson, I knew I had to have more. I dove into riding lessons with a joy I'd never felt before. I rode as much as I could.

Gradually, I got to know the other women at the barn, and I got to know the strength and determination that saw them through life's travails. I borrowed a helmet from a woman who had pulled herself back from the edge of death through multiple surgeries and the help of her horse—the bay mare I'd seen on that first day. I got to know an ovarian cancer survivor who threw herself so passionately into horses that no cancer would dare touch her. She now leaves bright red lipstick kisses on her horse's gray muzzle. I got to know women whose horses were the sweetest intimacies in their lives, women who had overcome severe injuries in order to ride again, women who freely gave their time, their expertise, their equipment, and their laughter to me, the newest rider at the barn.

I discovered that it had been more than just health insurance or antidepressants I had lacked when I first arrived at the stable on that summer day. It had been courage, resolve, and the willingness to work through exhaustion to do something that I loved. I had also lacked friendship. Living with depression and anemia had boxed me in. I had barely allowed myself to have acquaintances, and when I did, I flinched in fear of a sting or a barb. But at the barn I found support, common passion, and consuming joy. I found a place where women's faces became lined with barn dirt, not age, where makeup ran freely down cheeks, and where teasing insults were tossed lightly, without harm.

I went from a sheltered, quiet life with my depression to a life filled with vibrant teachers and friends who accepted me and encouraged me to do what I loved to do—ride, ride, and ride some more. That first lesson, walking stodgily along with Max, filled with strange sensations, set me on a path that is marked with milestones: my first fall and the months needed to heal, the first time I went riding without an instructor, my first trail ride, and my first independent canter in an arena lined with cheering, yelling, and waving friends, my husband smiling in the midst of them.

But it wasn't just the ride that set me on the path. It was that first instinct, after being hurt by the friend at church, to seek self-preservation in horses. It was that inner drive to go to the barn when I felt I needed healing. It was that incentive to overcome depression and to get better—no matter what it took— just so that I could ride. That was what gave me the strength to return to horses, breathe deeply of their scent, and feel the warmth radiate from their powerful bodies into my own.

—Harmony Marie Harrison

photography ©iStockphoto.com/Jeff Clow

My Pal

No one else could see us, and this was our preference. I was in Pal's stall, where he was lying down for a mid-morning nap. My heart was breaking and filled with sadness. Nestled in that cozy place where Pal's legs tucked beside him, supported by hooves, knees, and neck, I incoherently sobbed my troubles to Pal. He, in turn, held and comforted me. He accepted my tears and allowed them to soak into his soft palomino coat. Pal listened, looked at me with wise eyes, and dispelled my pain into the shafts of gentle sunlight around us. Looking back on that moment, I feel certain I wouldn't have survived without Pal. He was my closest friend.

I met Pal in the dead cold of February, just as I turned fourteen. The bottom had dropped out of my life. Grief over my grandmother's recent death consumed me. Grandma Evelyn had been my caretaker during early childhood and nurtured my interest in horses. She paid for my first riding lessons and snapped pictures of me at horse shows. As my riding abilities grew, she shrank from the cancer that eventually would kill her. My parents were less enthusiastic about my passion for what they considered an expensive hobby. They preferred that I join sports teams at school, and sometimes grounded me from horse activities. Without Grandma Evelyn's encouragement, I felt lost.

To assert my independence, I began a dangerous rebellion. I snuck out at night and ran away from home. I experimented with alcohol, cigarettes, purging, cutting, and hitting myself— anything to distract myself from my suffering. From the pit of my despair, I wrote dark poems and suicide notes. I was an angry adolescent, poisoned by self-loathing.

During this difficult time, I began to train horses. Pal had been a pony horse at a harness-racing track where they rescued runaway horses. When I began to work with him, all he knew was a prancing high-energy "whoa" and a fast-as-wildfire bolt. I taught him the basics and schooled him through a few shows and fairs. At the end of the summer, I was supposed to sell him—a simple commission job—except that I'd fallen in love with him. As I helped Pal cope with the stress of his equine education, he sheltered me from the hell that my life had become. I couldn't imagine living without him.

Things worsened that spring when my trainer had a falling out with Maple, the owner of the stable where Pal was boarded. My trainer left in a violent huff and wanted me to go with her. I was torn. I had followed her from barn to barn for years. Maple reassured me that I should do what felt right in my heart. She offered to buy Pal for me to lease and said I could work off his board. I trusted her and wanted to be with Pal, but it was hard to leave my trainer. Pal got me through the heartache while I made the decision to stay.

When things got too tough, we would take off down the road. Pal was fast and loved to run. I would lean forward and try to keep my eyes open, in spite of the wind that stung them to tears. As his galloping hooves pounded across miles of dirt road, I let go of my worries. Only at these times could I leave behind my melancholy rut of hopelessness. The adrenaline rush was bliss for us both and we would return to the barn hours later, reborn and refreshed.

Depression, bipolar disorder, and suicide were not uncommon in my family. While I knew something wasn't right, I didn't know the severity of the mental illness that challenged my mother and her sisters. I wondered whether I had inherited some gene that would cause me to self-destruct. It wasn't something we talked about at home, especially after my mother's postpartum depression, suicide attempt, and hospitalization years earlier. She had since stabilized on medication and flourished in newfound spirituality, but I still walked on egg-shells around her, fearing the confrontations sparked by my reckless behavior. I knew my parents loved me. I had all the privileges of a suburban upbringing, but I hated being home. Only at the barn could I let loose and be myself, feel accepted for who I was, and flee the expectations that exceeded my abilities. Pal let me be me.

Unable to relate to my parents, my trainer gone, and without Grandma's supportive presence, I sank deeper into despair and suicidal impulses. I felt worthless, so it was a boost to my low self-esteem when an older rider showed an interest in me. I ignored my friends and spent all my time with him, trail riding and talking horses. I wasn't yet in high school, but I felt mature riding home in his car after 4-H work sessions and drinking at parties with older kids. What I didn't see at the time was that he was emotionally disturbed. I didn't know his history of sexual violence against other girls and women in our rural community. My naiveté let me believe he liked me, but during my four-teenth summer he raped me repeatedly. Somehow I thought these forced, sometimes violent, sexual encounters were my fault. I already hated myself, now I also felt intense shame.

It was too much to endure alone, but my rapist threatened retaliation if I told anyone. I feared losing the respect of friends and losing my parents' permission to ride, but mostly I feared I wouldn't be believed. Trapped and immobilized by shame and fear, I let three years of silence pass before I told a person about my victimization, but Pal helped me bear the secret burden from the start. He heard my sorrow, empathized, and embraced me with an open heart. Almost daily we took rides that often covered twenty miles. I would pack a lunch and bring a halter so he could graze. I sang "We all ride on a yellow palomino" to him to the tune of the Beatles' "Yellow Submarine." I lost myself in fantasies of riding into the sunset and never coming back, heading west to carve out a new life, just me and my horse. Imagining a future far from the torment helped me through the events of our first year together.

Pal and I became close partners. We soared away from daily battles through jumping and dressage. The joy of riding him gave me a sense of lightness while the rest of my life spiraled into chaos. When I wasn't at the barn, I continued to self-destruct: I tried every drug available to me, developed an eating disorder, and sabotaged relationships with friends and boyfriends. Constantly, I thought about killing myself. A few times, too emotionally distraught to cope, I took too many painkillers or cut more deeply than usual.

I kept the blackest moments carefully hidden from friends and family. There was only Pal to comfort me, and he, I discovered, was more than enough. With the ever-present love of my horse, I lived through the nightmares of high school. To him I could bring my wounds and scars, admit my frailties, repent my irrational acting out, and feel loved in spite of the horrible person I thought I was. Pal sustained me with his gentle sense of humor and overflowing generosity of heart. When I most needed a friend, I would gaze deeply into his compassionate eyes, study my reflection on their surface, and then look deeper and wonder about the physical structures inside. Finally, I would concentrate deeper still to recognize the soul that was shining out from within. It was the soul of my healer, my Pal, and I felt comforted.

Eventually Pal developed arthritic hocks that ended our competitive riding. Several veterinarians recommended that he be semi-retired to easy trail riding, only as much as he could enjoy without pain. I wanted to keep and care for Pal, rather than find another show horse. Maple understood our unique bond and generously signed over his papers, making him officially mine.

During my freshman year of college, I moved Pal to a little barn closer to where I lived. He was the only horse and I was his sole caretaker. We spent happy years there, leisurely riding in the woods and enjoying one another's company. Taking care of my beloved friend was the highlight of every day. Each time I arrived at the barn, he would nicker a low, appreciative "wuh-huh-huh," a sound that melted my heart.

With Pal, I continued to heal as I entered young adulthood. No one could ever know me as well as he did. We parted ways when I began graduate school. He went to a good home where he would be ridden occasionally by a young girl. I could see him whenever I wanted, so I knew he was content. Although I missed him, I was ready to move on knowing he was now a source of healing for a new family.

I chose a career in counseling so that I could help others who are struggling. Naturally, I think of horses as partners in the healing process. I became certified in equine-assisted psychotherapy so that I could offer activities with horses to clients coping with mental health or personal growth issues. As a certified therapeutic riding instructor, I also teach people with physical, developmental, emotional, and mental challenges how to ride and interact with horses. I always marvel at the emotions that horses help humans to feel. These intuitive, genuine, and caring animals are eager to help us grow. I have great mentors—both two- and four-legged—to guide me as I grow professionally and personally.

I've come full circle from those days of secretly crying in a stall with my horse. Just as Pal helped me, I now help others. He was a model for me in the healing process, and I can never repay my debt to him. But he doesn't expect repayment; he's just glad to have been part of my journey. I will always love Pal and always feel his presence—he is the foundation of my path to healing.

—Heather Hoffman

No Longer Seeking Sandpipers

When I was twenty-one, I started having laryngitis. Then my fingers wouldn't work. I noticed it most around my horse, Sandpiper. I rode Western, and I couldn't lift the saddle onto her. While cantering,

I'd suddenly slip off. Hearing my "Whoa!" she would stop. I'd pull myself back up, but then it would happen again.

The doctor diagnosed myasthenia gravis, a progressive neurological illness that causes all the muscles to become weak to the point of not functioning. In a matter of weeks, I could hardly talk, walk, or lift anything. Others had to care for Sandpiper, and her routine changed drastically. No more trail rides. While I became housebound, she became barn bound.

Long before Sandpiper, I had prepared for the day when I might have a horse of my own. That day came when I was fifteen. Sandpiper was a smart, eight-month-old mix of Anglo-Arab, quarter horse, and appaloosa—a little bit of each and all mine. I knew that she had to be two years old before I could ride her, so I waited. In the meantime, I introduced her to my world. We explored apple orchards, turkey and pig farms, parking lots, shopping centers, and car washes.

Every morning she greeted me with a nicker when I arrived to feed her. She even learned my schedule and slept late on weekends. In her stall I'd lie next to her, stroking her as she slowly awoke and stretched to the sound of my voice. I was in horse heaven.

Finally she turned two—a tall, gorgeous chestnut with a full appaloosa blanket, narrow blaze, and flaxen mane and tail. We took our first ride together in her field. I climbed up on her back. She nuzzled my left foot and started walking. Suddenly she took off at a slow, relaxed canter up the small hill and came to a stop at the top. I hugged her neck. She nuzzled my foot again and off we galloped back down the hill. I thanked her, slid off, and life was great for six years.

Then I became ill.

A few months after my diagnosis, my doctor gave me a medication that seemed to help. I couldn't wait to visit Sandpiper.

At first sight we ran calling to each other. But then she backed away and sniffed me. She could see and smell that I was not the same. I was clumsy, so brushing now irritated her. Saddling and bridling became painful to us both. She would bite at the saddle as I shimmied it up her side. I apologized, and she laid her ears back. It took two hours or more to tack her up. When riding, I needed both hands to hold on.

Some days I could ride, but I could only make it about 500 feet from the barn before falling forward onto her neck. Sandpiper would stop and wait as I struggled back into position. Often this process took fifteen or thirty minutes. Then I'd ask her to walk again and turn around back to the barn. It took another two hours of struggle to unsaddle, groom, and feed her.

On one of those short rides from the barn, Sandpiper abruptly stopped and refused to go forward. The more I urged her, the more agitated she became. Suddenly Sandpiper reared up about a foot. I froze. So did she. I urged her again, and she reared higher. The she lowered her head, swung it to my left leg, and bargained to go back to her barn. I urged her once more. Up she went even higher. When Sandpiper came down she swung her head back to my left ankle as if to say, *It's the barn, or I go higher!* Finally, I accepted her message.

A week later I tried to ride Sandpiper again. We had only gotten across the barnyard before she suddenly reared again and again, swinging her head back and forth, wringing her tail, and pawing the ground. Out of sheer terror, I begged her to stop, and at last she quieted. Slowly I slid off and led her back to her barn.

I never rode Sandpiper again. During this time I was in and out of emergency rooms and hospitals. The doctors decided I needed surgery. A year after the surgery, I was so weak that my family talked me into giving up my horse. Devastated, I called Judy, the woman who had sold her to me. Judy made me a deal that changed my life.

She wanted me to trade Sandpiper for another mare. Music Lou was seven years old and untrained, but had a calmer, kinder temperament than Sandpiper. Because I knew Judy loved Sandpiper and would take wonderful care of her, and because I could not imagine life without a horse, I agreed.

Six months later, Sandpiper left, and Music Lou arrived. When I peeked into her trailer, my heart sank. With her huge head, plate-size hooves, and wide, deep chest, this mare looked like a miniature draft horse. The only pretty things about her were her mane and tail, black and full, and her body color, a rich mahogany bay. She had none of the refinement and style of my Sandpiper.

Music Lou's eyes widened in terror as three men tried to unload her. They grabbed the ropes attached to her heavy halter and dragged her, rearing and plunging, down the ramp. Hadn't Judy said "calmer and kinder"? This horse was wild!

Somehow the men managed to get her into our round corral. After they left, Lou stood trembling against the far side of the corral, the whites of her eyes showing wide with fear. I left her alone to calm down and headed straight to the phone.

"Music Lou is very well bred," said Judy, holding steady against my onslaught of questions. "Her sire, Music Mount, was multi-talented in the reining world, and her dam, Taxi Bubba Lou, was a proven producer of reiners who had done well herself."

Then came the bad news.

"When I got her she was a range-grown three-year-old," Judy continued, "not handled at all except for annual veterinary procedures. I sent her to a renowned trainer in Stockton. Lou was supposed to be there a month, but she only lasted two weeks. The problem was her extreme fear of humans. At one point the trainer was trying to get a saddle on her when she broke away and ran straight through a fence made of railroad tie posts and solid steel pipe. Later, when he attempted to get her into a horse trailer, she panicked and kicked it almost apart. After that, I turned her loose on several hundred acres with other horses and she's been there for the last four years."

There was silence. While Judy waited for my next question, I asked myself two big ones. Could I ride this homely, crazy mare? And could she ever give me the bond I'd had with Sandpiper?

Every day for the next two weeks, I sat in a chair near Lou's corral. Talking and singing, I tossed carrots, apples, and hay in her direction. Making any sound was difficult for me. The muscles in my mouth and throat would stop working and I'd have to rest for several minutes before starting again.

In a month I moved the chair into the corral. A month later Lou walked up to me and took food from my hand. Then I started carrying a halter and lead rope. Sometimes I sat, and sometimes I stood, but always talking, singing, and tossing tidbits to her. She began accepting changes faster. At the same time, my coordination began to improve.

Still, I was weak. My mother handed me things and helped me lift. Three months after Lou's arrival, I could lead her, brush her, and clean her hooves. Due to my poor physical condition, I opted for an English saddle, much lighter than Western. My horse didn't care. She took off as soon as she saw me coming with this contraption.

The first time Mom and I put the saddle on her, she bucked so high, it landed outside the corral. So we just touched her with it, lightly at first. Soon we could set it on her back. Mom would hold it in place while I led her slowly around. We did a little more every day. Finally we could fasten the girth.

Six months after Lou's arrival I thought she was ready for me to get on. I had not been on a horse since that last painful ride on Sandpiper. I was frightened, having already seen how emotional and physical this horse could be. But something in those big brown eyes—the softest eyes I've ever known—told me it would be okay.

When Mom tried to talk me out of it, I reassured her with a plan: Lou was used to seeing me sit in a chair. Maybe I could stand on it, and try just leaning on her. The problem was that I still had not recovered my balance.

My mother helped me up on the chair and held me there as I stood, clucking softly to Lou. To our utter amazement, she walked right over to me, nickered low, and nuzzled into my hands.

After that, Mom would get me set up on the chair, and I'd call to Lou. We'd get her to follow a carrot around the chair until she was lined up in front of me. Then I'd act like I was mounting. Following several weeks of this, I put my foot in the stirrup for the first time. Lou didn't budge. Next I tried to pull myself up, with Mom pushing me from behind. The horse never moved. She seemed to understand that I needed her to be still.

Then fear swept through me. If Lou reared, I knew I'd never ride again. *Now or never.*

My mother gave me a push and made my dream real. For the first time in three years, I was on top of the world.

A month later Music Lou and I set off on our first competitive trail ride. I worried that someone would notice I was slow and inadequate, but she held me up. If I started to fall, she'd shift her weight to catch me as I took hold of her mane.

Judges marked our scores at several obstacles on the thirty-mile trip. Lou remained steady past snorting pigs and barking dogs. When we dismounted and remounted in the middle of the ride, she allowed me to steady myself with her tail and leg. We placed sixth out of thirty horses and riders.

Sandpiper had been my drop-dead beauty, but in plain and plodding Music Lou I found what I had sought and what I thought I had lost forever—a friend who accepted me no matter what. Had it not been for Lou, I'd probably still be seeking Sandpipers.

—Barbara O'Connor

My Special Olympians

Friday morning of Memorial Day weekend came early, the red-streaked Texas dawn filtering through the curtains of our third-floor hotel room. Still groggy, my husband and I made our way down-stairs and helped ourselves to the hotel's compli-mentary breakfast. Balancing plastic containers of cereal, sweet rolls, juice, and coffee, we migrated toward others dressed in our group's uniform of the day: jeans or shorts, dirt-stained boots, and gray T-shirts bearing a royal blue emblem of a child hugging a horse. Several gulps of coffee later, our excitement level rose as we looked forward to the day ahead.

Early the previous morning, our caravan, including two pick-ups straining against the weight of loaded horse trailers, had headed north from Houston. We arrived mid-afternoon at the JJ Expo Center in Rockwall, east of Dallas. The unremitting wind swirled dust in our eyes as we unpacked our gear, prepared stalls, and schooled the horses. Dinner was late and bedtime even later, but nobody complained. We were proud to be counted among the loyal crew of staff and volunteers assisting our team of riders at the 2002 State Special Olympics.

Until I began volunteering with a local therapeutic riding center, I didn't even know the Special Olympics included equestrian events. Large, unpredictable animals and riders with disabilities seemed unlikely partners for a competitive venue. To the uninitiated it looked like a recipe for disaster. But I soon witnessed what an amazing combination a horse and "special" rider can make.

My curiosity about therapeutic riding developed over several years as I regularly came across special-interest news stories about the center in our area and read their frequent requests for volunteers. Finally one summer I suggested to my husband that we give it a try.

In those first few months of volunteering, I learned as much about myself as I did about the riders and horses. The clients included children with Down syndrome, autism, and various combinations of learning and physical disabilities. Some of the adult riders were paraplegics, recovering brain-injury or stroke patients, or people with multiple sclerosis.

The first thing I learned was that these very special equestrians were amazingly courageous. Give them a task—whether as "simple" as holding the reins with uncooperative fingers or as complicated as steering a horse through a series of obstacles— and they respond with pride and determination.

I also learned that each horse contributes its own element of magic to the mix. Some instinctively shift their weight to balance an unsteady rider. Others have infinite patience with fidgeting legs or erratic tugs on the reins. The calmest ones earn the reputation of "bombproof." Those are the ones that never blink an eye when a child bangs a noisy toy against their necks or clips clothespins to their manes.

Finally I learned that behind each rider is a steadfast family support system. No matter how tedious and trying they may find their day-to-day care responsibilities, these families are always *there* in body and spirit.

And we certainly felt like one large and wonderful family that Friday morning in Rockwall, when our team of ten riders, coaching staff, and numerous volunteers assembled behind our blue-and-white team banner for the Special Olympics opening ceremonies. Smiling broadly, we marched through the clumpy, red-brown dirt of the arena and took our place in a massive rainbow, our royal blue intermingling with the other teams' bright red, flamboyant turquoise, vivid green, and myriad shades in between.

Hundreds of voices—some strong, some hesitant, and some stridently enthusiastic—joined in the Pledge of Allegiance and the athletes' Special Olympics Oath. The Olympic "torch," fashioned from aluminum foil atop a short wooden staff, made its way along the procession of athletes. Finally the announcer spoke the words we'd all been waiting for: "Let the games begin!"

Back at the horse stalls, confusion reigned as parents made sure the riders' collars were straight, buttons buttoned, boots polished, and helmets secure. Mount leaders gave their horses last-minute grooming touch-ups and checked and rechecked tack. We breathed in the smells of wood shavings, horse manure, fly spray, as well as the inescapable dust whipped up by the wind.

My rider, George, who is hearing impaired, competed first in Western equitation on Gem, a gray appaloosa with a jog-trot as comfortable as a back-porch glider. George had hovered outside Gem's stall, making sure I didn't forget show pad, reins, or stirrup lengths. With rider mounted, we plodded into the outdoor warm-up arena, where the sun turned the plowed earth into a shimmering, blinding sea. Both of us squinting, we practiced walk-halt and walk-jog transitions, did some circles and reverses, and reviewed what George could expect in his equitation class. After some final reminders from the coach, I escorted horse and rider to the competition arena. The announcer's amplified voice reverberated through the cavernous interior as he introduced each competitor.

With the lead rope knotted loosely around Gem's neck, I stayed just close enough to ensure Gem's proper and safe behavior and to relay the judge's instructions to George, who was eagerly waiting. Like a pro, George reined his horse at a walk and jog, while I labored to keep pace through the ankle-deep dirt. When the ring steward asked the riders to line up in front of the judge, I did my subtle best to keep both George and Gem quiet and focused. The judge worked her way down the row and asked the riders to demonstrate their skills in backing their horse. Again, George and Gem gave a flawless performance.

Then, more waiting while the results were tallied. As the awards were announced in reverse order, I silently repeated, "Don't call George's name yet." As dearly as if I were competing myself, I coveted that gold medal for my rider's impressive performance.

"Third place goes to George Singleton," came the announcement. I gave George an elated thumbs-up as the ring steward tramped through the dirt to drape the bronze medal around his neck. He held it up and grinned as his gaze searched the applauding spectators for his mom's special smile.

Later, George received fifth place in working trail, and his four-man drill team earned silver medals. I couldn't have been prouder. In fact, I often had to blink back tears—tears that *weren't* caused by the blowing dust—as I watched all the athletes step up to the awards platform at the end of each day's competition. At Special Olympics, every competitor receives an award, and it's obvious that ribbon or medal, first place or last, what matters most is the chance to stand proudly in front of family and friends and be recognized as much for the effort as for the achievement.

It's too bad the rest of the world hasn't learned the Special Olympics definition of winning. I watch the "real" Olympics and cringe as the commentators interview the silver- or bronze-medal winners and ask them how it feels to "lose." *Lose*, when they've conquered unimaginable obstacles just to earn the right to compete at the Olympic level? It makes me ponder my own motives and goals. Do I really need to be better than everyone else in my career field, in sports, or other endeavors? Beyond their cheerfulness, their artless sincerity, and their courage and determination, my Special Olympians have taught me that what matters most in life is being the very best "me" I can be.

Thanks, George and Gem, for reminding me what life is truly all about.

—Myra Langley Johnson

Competitive Spirit

I fell in love during our first encounter. His large, almond-shaped eyes were the color of roasted coffee beans. His facial expression was soft and gentle, with a small hint of impishness. His chest muscles glistened with definition; it was apparent that he worked hard to maintain his muscular physique. His height intimidated me, but I sensed from his polite demeanor that he might be a suitable partner.

Borage was a sixteen-hand bay Thoroughbred that had raced in France for five years before coming to California to train as a hunter/jumper. I was a novice rider who had recently been diagnosed with multiple sclerosis. Even though my doctors had warned me that my activity level would be curtailed, I was having a hard time accepting that. I had played competitive sports all of my life. I had been a USTA-ranked tennis player. Now facing symptoms including fatigue, numbness, loss of vision, even paralysis, the diagnosis was proving a huge blow to me physically, mentally, and emotionally. I'm just not cut out to be a bridge player, but I began to have second thoughts about horseback riding.

"Okay, come to the mounting block and I'll help you get on," called Cindy Freeman, the owner, trainer, and resident horse whisperer of Mission Hills Equestrian Center in Fremont, California. She was the one who convinced me to try riding as a way to stay physically active despite my illness. Since moving next door to Cindy, I had visited her frequently. I learned how to groom the horses, but otherwise I didn't know anything about them. I had certainly never been on one, and now I could feel the tension rising through my body.

"I'm terrified," I said. "Are you going to hold the lead rope the whole time? I can't see very well in the arena. What if I lose my balance?" I assailed her with questions. Cindy didn't answer; she was looking at the chaps she had lent me to protect my legs.

"I think you need to rearrange your riding apparel," she said. I glanced down at my half chaps and was embarrassed to realize that the zipper was on the inside of my calf instead of the outside. Earlier that morning I had paraded my new riding clothes proudly around the equestrian center. None of the experienced riders had mentioned that my chaps were on backwards.

After the adjustment, Cindy led Borage to the block and helped me mount. Because of the MS, my balance and vision are poor, so I felt like a toddler taking her first steps. But Cindy was reassuring and confident. "Don't worry about your vision, Borage will help you. He's the one responsible for navigating the path, not you. Sit deep in the saddle and keep a loose rein. Eventually you won't have to think so much about all the details and riding will become second nature." I wanted to believe her.

She led us around the arena a few times, and then I was on my own. She reminded me to take advantage of my well-developed competitive skills. "I think you'll be able to sustain the muscle tone you've already got in your legs if you continue riding. You'll also gain some upper-body strength." Those were the words I needed to hear to keep me going.

I have accomplished a lot in my life. After my divorce, I advanced my career from sales secretary to chief executive officer of an office products company before retiring early, partly because of the multiple sclerosis. As a single parent I raised three children and several dogs. An avid gardener and gourmet cook, I spent many hours on my ranch growing wine grapes, vegetables, and a variety of beautiful flowers for cutting. Competition has always been a part of who I was, and my disease threatened the intense drive that had facilitated my achievements to date. At first, I'd been in denial about the MS, telling myself, "This isn't going to happen to me," even as I started to see signs of deterioration. My vision would come and go, and my coordination was affected. Cindy's words gave me hope that, despite the symptoms, there was a chance I could stay active and competitive. After that first lesson, I knew she was a special person with a tremendous amount of patience and love. Still, riding would turn out to be the hardest sport I ever learned.

For a year, Cindy spent one day a week training me to ride Borage. We called these my "therapy sessions." I spent another three days a week at her ranch riding on my own to develop strength, balance, and endurance. Gradually Borage and I learned to trust each other. I became a little less fearful and more assertive, and he became a little gentler. Borage is naturally affectionate, and sometimes when I groomed him he would stretch his head back and rest his soft chin on my shoulder. When I was riding, he seemed to sense I wasn't all there and took good care of me. I learned that I could reveal weaknesses to Borage that I couldn't bring myself to show anyone else. He became my secret confidant and we developed a solid bond.

In the spring, Cindy convinced me to enter a local English pleasure riding show. At least I knew how to put my chaps on this time. I also had confidence in Borage and knew I could handle the jitters so I thought, "Why not?"

When we arrived at the show, I saw no other senior citizens participating in the novice class. The average age was about fourteen. I wanted to run and hide in the horse trailer. I confronted Cindy, "I know I weigh only ninety-eight pounds, but surely someone will discover that there's a little old lady under this velvet helmet!"

"This will be good for you," she replied. "Now turn around so I can tie the entry number on your back."

The judge called the fifteen entrants in the walk/trot class into the arena. I took a deep breath and tried to contain my excitement. Cindy perched on the rail and prepared to coach me during the competition. I took comfort in her presence because I was worried about posting on the correct diagonal during the trot exercise. Borage moved so smoothly, it was hard for me to know when to lift myself in the saddle. This had been a weak spot for me during training, and I knew if I failed to get it right during the show, I wouldn't be eligible for an award. Secretly I hoped to capture fourth or fifth place.

The class performed the exercises as a group. I tried to concentrate on the basics that Cindy had taught me, but there were too many things to think about. The judge asked us to walk, trot, and halt, and at times I had to maneuver Borage around other horses that weren't moving at our pace. An eternity passed before the class finally ended. By that point, I was mentally and physically exhausted.

The judge asked all the equestrians to line up in the center of the arena and face the grandstand. Beginning with fifth place, he announced the winners. When he got to second place, I knew I had not won an award. There were many others with more experience, and they all seemed so young and fearless. We listened for the announcement of the first-place winner.

"First place goes to number two-thirty-one."

All the riders looked straight ahead, but the winner didn't ride forward. He announced the number again, to no avail.

The person next to me asked, "What's your number?" I didn't remember. She stretched sideways to look and said, "You're number two-thirty-one!" I looked over at Cindy, and her wide smile confirmed that I had indeed won. Beaming, I attached the blue ribbon to Borage's bridle.

The event proved to me that competition was still in my blood. With Borage's help, we won two more blue ribbons that day: one in the equitation class where I was judged on my skills as a rider, and another in the walk/trot pleasure class where Borage was judged on his ability to listen and perform. Later when I asked Cindy how we had managed to win, she just smiled and said, "Sometimes everything just comes together."

—Jody McPheeters

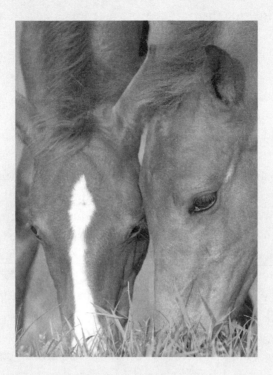

Cutter, Peppy, and Me

I can't pretend that I always loved horses, even though I grew up next door to them. I would hang on the wooden fence that bordered our properties and watch them play, roll on the ground, and sometimes get stuck upside down in the irrigation ditch. I didn't ride them; they were racehorses and they smelled funny.

When I was around seven, my mother woke me early one morning, and we walked across the dew-soaked grass to see a mare give birth to a foal. Two spindly front legs, followed by the rest of the slimy body, slid out the back end of the mare. I was amazed and disgusted at the same time. I watched in silence, not out of fear of disturbing the mare, but more because I didn't want to break the spell of being alone with my mother. We had recently watched my cat give birth right under my bed. Here we were, the two of us with none of my brothers in sight, watching another miracle take place. Other than those few experiences and that memorable moment, I had little contact with horses.

As I grew, I hung on the fence less and looked at boys more. When my parents asked if I wanted to take riding lessons or modeling, I choose modeling.

At the age of forty-four, I found myself single again. As in many divorce stories, I reacted by doing something completely out of character: I bought a red Miata and a horse I couldn't ride. The car was too small and the horse threw my eight-year-old daughter. I sold both impulse purchases.

Two years later I inherited two horses from another failed relationship. Peppy was a striking twenty-one-year-old mare from the King Ranch in Texas. Cutter was a fourteen-year-old red roan gelding that had only been ridden on Sundays by an elderly gentleman. I found a barn that would take us in. At first glance, it looked rustic and unkempt. I soon discovered that appearances were deceiving.

The River Bend Ranch was full of love and felt like home. My little shitzu, Ruby, became a "barn dog." Girls between the ages of nine and eighteen frequented the place and spent hours grooming and riding. I noticed a change in my daughter, as she began to act the way kids are supposed to act at that age. At the barn, she wasn't concerned about who said what or what she was wearing. I noticed, too, that I liked the way I felt around the horses. I began cleaning my own stalls and shooing away the stall cleaner if he ventured near with his apple picker and wheelbarrow.

I loved talking about horses with Jan, who was the barn owner and my trainer. I would follow her around asking question after question while she fed the herd. She would point to a particular horse and say, "See how he stands with one foot forward?" I would look with my untrained eye and pretend to see what she saw and say yes. "We need to see if there's an abscess in his hoof." Jan would run her hand down the horse's right front tendon to feel for heat and then check his left front and compare. She would make me do the same. And so it went day after day, learning, teaching, and sharing. At the time, I was studying psychology in graduate school. Jan and I would talk about relationships between people and horses. I began to notice how some people were just like horses in the way they moved and responded to other people. I felt as though I was becoming more and more like a horse.

Away from the barn, I felt anxious about life's challenges. Now as soon as I parked my car under the shade of the giant mesquite tree, my horses would call out their greeting and the rest of the world would fall away. My wardrobe changed to jeans, T-shirt, and ponytail. I quit going to traditional talk therapy and went to the barn instead. I was officially horse crazy at the age of forty-eight.

Three years later, I completed my master's degree in expressive arts therapy. I opened a small private practice, and now I often meet my clients at the barn. Usually I bring my traveling studio of art and music supplies, including giant pads of drawing paper, oil pastels, tempera paints, brushes, beads, feathers, and percussive instruments. People come to me fragmented and lost. My horses, the arts, and I help them see their place in the world and become better humans.

Sometimes a client will stand in the round pen with one of my horses or groom a horse using only her hands. Tears roll down her face as profound insights occur. Poems emerge, paintings are created, and sometimes lives are transformed. The client often leaves with a clearer heart, new hope for a more fulfilled life, and the insight that comes from an extraordinary place. They leave ready to return again to uncover yet another layer of what life has dealt them. Through all this, I witness compassion from my mare, Peppy, as she consoles a client grieving a beloved pet, or a woman who suffered sexual abuse as a child, or children who aren't able to express themselves in traditional therapy. My horses are always present and willing to help people reclaim their lives.

One client, Sylvia, came to work through her sexual abuse issues. She was unable to trust anyone in a relationship. I asked her to step into the round pen with Cutter while I watched from outside the pen. Cutter immediately came toward her and began to nuzzle her chest, moving her backward around the pen. He continued this for some time. As I watched the 1,000-pound animal push the 140-pound woman, she began to cry. I asked her to step outside the pen, sit in the shade, and write about what had just taken place.

Sylvia came to the conclusion that, once again, her boundaries were being violated. She was familiar with this feeling around men, and now she felt it with a horse. She cried, and I asked her to return to the pen. This time, her behavior was markedly different. She lunged Cutter on a long line in the direction she wanted him to go. As she recognized the significance of her actions, tears flowed down her cheeks once more. Later in a poem about her experience she wrote, "Tears flowing/You pushed me again/This time in horse form/No longer will this be allowed/I stand to face you/Horse-human/Back off, I am back." Creating her art helped her continue her experience with the horse and brought it to another form of communication. The art allowed Sylvia to observe and shape her transformation.

In the following session, Sylvia used the language of her imagination through poetry and painting, and later talked about her visual imagery. The art contained the intensity of her emotion, yet allowed her to reflect upon it later. During our last session, Sylvia wanted to see all her artwork, poetry, and reflections at the same time. We spread the pieces on the tack room floor and commented on her visual diary, reliving the words she had spoken and the breakthroughs she had felt. It was clear that she had made remarkable progress toward a healthier and more authentic life. Through it all, the horses had helped her crystallize her creative efforts.

Sylvia discovered that she could now own her suffering—and release it. We celebrated together and danced around the pile of drawings, poems, and journal entries. Then we led the horses through the maze of artwork that they had helped her create. At last, Sylvia burned the images and writings.

As clients find their way to me and to my horses, the work that unfolds often surprises them—and me. The horses and I move between the seen and unseen worlds in an organic dance, allowing the client to address more quickly the problem at hand. At times I feel I am a portal. I provide a safe space for exploration and a sacred space for possibility. My horses respond to my clients with a knowing sense and listen to them in a way that no one has listened to them before. These people experience a sense of coming home to themselves, helped by the wisdom of the horse.

Often I find myself hanging over the fence, just as I did as a little girl, watching the horses roll, lick, chew, and tend to each other. The difference now is that I'm aware of the effect they have on me while they unfold their magic. Today, I love the way they smell. My mother would be amused at this life that has found me and thrilled that all those modeling lessons didn't go to waste. My posture is perfect when I'm riding my mare.

—Rebecca Paradies

Beautiful Silence

I first met Carol when I started taking riding lessons at a stable that didn't mind forty-five-year-old beginners. At least twice a week, she brought her granddaughter for lessons. We struck up an e-mail friendship because we shared a love of horses and because communication with Carol was so much easier that way. That was because Carol was almost totally deaf. She told me she had slowly begun to lose her hearing many years earlier, after contracting meningitis when her seventh child was a baby. Her hearing loss had progressed, and at sixty-five her world was filled with silence and frustration.

Although she was proud of her children and grandchildren, and she spoke fondly of birthday and holiday gatherings, Carol told me that she longed to go back to the days before she got sick. She missed the everyday sounds of her children's voices and the first cries of her grandchildren. Away from the loving sanctuary of her family, Carol felt lost and lonely. Only in the barn where the kittens played atop the hay and the horses nodded in their stalls did Carol feel she belonged.

Our friendship grew when Carol began taking riding lessons, too. Unexpectedly, a friend gave us a seventeen-year-old Thoroughbred named Piper to share. He was beautiful and so tall that when Carol stood on one side of him, I couldn't see the top of her blonde head from the other. But I could hear her tender voice and knew what she was saying without listening too hard: "Beautiful boy, sweet boy . . . you don't care that I can't hear you." She told me that when he nuzzled her neck his warm breath reminded her of a gentle melody.

I soon discovered that Piper had an amazing sixth sense when it came to Carol. He respected her and loved her unconditionally. He also took away the language barrier that surrounded her in the human world. With him she felt none of the pressure to try to hear and respond to what others said. He listened to her, and his body language spoke in ways that she could easily understand. With Piper, Carol wasn't deaf. Piper was her lifeline. When she was riding, Carol experienced a freedom and independence that spilled over into her everyday life. As she groomed and cared for Piper, my once-reserved friend found new confidence and strength. I marveled as she overcame obstacles and faced challenges on a daily basis. Others noticed, too. Our local newspaper published a story about her titled, "Rider Overcomes Hurdles to Face Life's Challenges." It should have read, "Horse Helps Rider Overcome Hurdles to Face Life's Challenges."

Frequently I'd see Piper nudge my dear friend as if to say, *It's time Carol, let's go!* Even though the trails in the ravine behind the barn were steep, Carol trusted Piper to take care of her. In the spring and summer, Carol's other senses took over: she smelled the lovely wildflowers, and she noticed the tiniest of details. People always rushed Carol, but Piper didn't. He allowed her to breathe life from their trail rides. She also took remarkable photographs from his steady back. Photo after photo offered windows to her world and revealed her talent: dew on long blades of grass, tiny eggs layered on green leaves, fawns with their mothers. The pictures spoke the emotion that she felt in her silence.

Winter was difficult for Carol. When the weather was bad, it was hard for her to get to the farm and even harder for her to ride. Snow and ice made her nervous. Sometimes she had to park her car at the end of the driveway, where it wouldn't get stuck, and trudge the long distance to the barn. Carol told me that keeping Piper in the arena, which was easier for her to reach, would break his spirit. She didn't want his spirit broken as hers had been.

I often watched Carol and Piper carry on private conversations. One winter day, as snowflakes began to fall, I listened as she curried her horse's already glistening winter coat and asked, "What do you think, fella?" I wondered if she could possibly be planning to ride outside of the safety of the arena. The footing on the trails would be treacherous, though others did it all the time. The thought of a winter ride terrified me, and I knew Carol's fears were greater than mine. "If she can do it, I can do it," I thought. It wasn't the first time that she had inspired me, and it wouldn't be the last. I busied myself with another horse while Carol pulled on her barn boots and chaps. "You'll take care of me, won't you, sweet boy?" she asked Piper as if she already knew the answer. The horse stood motionless, watching her. "It's almost as though he's reading my lips," she said to me. Piper whinnied his agreement.

Swiftly Carol opened the tack room door and got Piper's pad, saddle, and girth. The weight of the load caused her to stumble slightly. She secured the saddle in place like the expert horse-woman she had become. One more trip to the tack room, and she came back wearing her helmet and carrying a bridle. Out of the corner of my eye I watched her toss the reins over Piper's neck and gently place the bit in his mouth.

I settled into my saddle and waited for Carol to mount. Piper walked out the barn door and took his natural lead. Even though the snow was slowing down, silent, heavy flakes continued to paste themselves to the grass, the fence, and the bushes. They blanketed the trees. The trails ahead of us were carpeted in soft, white snow.

Carol told me later that she had expected to feel butterflies in her stomach, but there were none. Any other horse might have been impatient, but Piper was not. He waited until his rider was ready. Carol's hearing loss caused more than missed communication—it also created safety issues like compromised balance. She took plenty of time to square herself in the saddle. When she felt secure, she squeezed Piper's sides just a little and asked him to move on. "Such a good, good boy," she murmured as they began to make their way down the winding trail. "Such a good boy."

Piper walked slowly, sensing Carol's position, and I saw him shift his body in an effort to keep her balanced. I was still nervous, but Carol's confidence in Piper calmed us both. She saw the ravine and the woods as she had not seen them in the spring, summer, or autumn, yet she was not afraid. A squirrel darted across the path, chattering as it ran up an oak tree. Piper pointed one of his ears in the squirrel's direction and the other ear toward his rider. *My ears are your ears,* he seemed to say. *I'll keep you safe.* Carol understood.

Slowly, cautiously, we made our way across the frozen creek bed and up to the meadow. The snow began to fall harder. The cold, wet flakes made Carol's glowing face turn rosier still. I saw Piper stop and raise his head.

"Good boy, pretty boy," said Carol, "What are you doing?" And before I knew, she knew. A herd of grazing deer surrounded them. The deer used their muzzles to brush away the heavy snow and expose the last of the autumn grass. Time stood still. I felt like an intruder as I watched my friend and her horse become one with the beautiful wild creatures. Squirrels chirruped in the distance, a crow cawed, and Piper whinnied. I saw Carol smile, and I knew that her heart heard the sweet familiar sounds.

As long shadows stretched their fingers across the meadow, Carol squeezed Piper's sides and reluctantly asked him to move on. There was no question in my mind that when Carol was with Piper, her life of silence seemed beautiful, and the rest of the world seemed gentle and peaceful, just as it should be.

Three years ago, Carol was diagnosed with pancreatic cancer, and although she never rode Piper again, I knew that he still rekindled her spirit. Even in her last days, news of Piper brought a smile to her lips. Shortly after her diagnosis, Carol died peacefully.

Not long after Carol became ill, Piper's health began to fail, too. It was clear that he missed their special bond, and it became increasingly evident that no one else could fill the void in his life left by his friend. Piper passed away shortly after his dear companion died.

There is no doubt that the healing bond between horse and human exists. Carol and Piper were, for me, a shining example. I often think of that moment when they stood silently in the softly falling snow, surrounded by deer. In this memory, my friend and our horse live on forever.

—Jan Mader

How Jenny Can Ride

I drove the twenty miles to Crescent Hills Hunt Club with care. The golden light of the early summer evening cast long shadows on the lawns of the estates and slanted through the towering elm and maple trees that formed a canopy over the curving road. It was the

photography ©iStockphoto.com/AVTG

trunks of those large trees I watched closely. I made mental notes of the big, solid ones close to the road. It would be dark when I drove home, and it would be easy to make it look like I'd hit one by accident.

The Hunt Club may have been the most elite equestrian facility in the richest part of town, but when I emerged wearily from my car, I was greeted by the same horsy smells I remembered from my own modest barn: shavings, manure, hay, sweet feed, dirt, horses, and fresh evening air. The aroma immediately summoned memories of my beloved chestnut mare. I felt strangely comforted and yet sad at the same time, remembering how my spirits soared when I sat on her back and how I had cried for weeks when she was sold so I could attend college. Five years had gone by, but the ache of loss and longing felt as strong as ever—perhaps stronger, given my current state of discouragement and hopelessness over the general direction of my life. "Don't cry—come on! Take a deep breath. Horses first, then suicide." It made perfect sense at the time.

A dirt access road led me between the stables and white-fenced riding arenas, and I soon met a woman who held a chunky appaloosa next to a stock trailer. "I'm a new volunteer," I said. "Could you tell me who Tina is? We spoke on the phone a few days ago."

The woman smiled. "Glad to have you! I'm Charlotte, and Tina is unloading some of our other horses." She gestured toward a solid, sun-weathered woman who held a smallish chestnut gelding by the halter as he stepped out of the trailer. "Tina! We have a new volunteer!"

"I'm so glad you came, Kristen," said Tina. "You have horse experience, right? Here, this is Red." She handed me the chestnut's lead rope. "Take him inside, and we'll bring you some tack."

I led him through large sliding doors into a well-lit, spacious arena. Red turned his head to examine me—a stranger. I scratched his poll while he gave my jacket pockets a good snuffle. I smiled. "Sorry, nothing in there, buddy." I smoothed his neck and curled my fingers into his mane, which was pulled short enough that it wouldn't quite lie down. "I didn't realize I missed this so much." I blinked back tears again.

Remembering the tack, I looked toward the open doors. A small group of adults and children waited on a raised observation deck next to the arena. I wondered what their stories were. Some were in wheelchairs, others in leg braces; one boy had Down syndrome; and a man carried a thin girl wearing a seizure helmet. They all looked eagerly at the horses. Suddenly I felt embarrassed in front of them. I thought of the rejection letters that had told me I wouldn't be considered for the teaching jobs I'd desperately wanted. I thought of my job at a daycare center, which I despised. "How can I stand here and be anything but thankful?"

A man walked toward me with an English saddle and bridle. "Is this Red?"

"Is that his tack?" The man nodded. I waited for him to put the saddle on, but he stood looking at me. "Would you like me to tack him up?" I asked.

"I think you'd better," he said. "I try to help when my daughter rides, but I really don't know much about horses."

"If you hold the horse, I'll take the tack," I said as I handed him the lead rope. I put the saddle on Red and adjusted his saddle pad and girth to be comfortable. He took a deep breath to keep the girth loose, but I remembered that trick and snuck back to tighten it a couple more holes. Red turned his head in annoyance. "You can't fool me, mister," I said to him, with a pat on his neck. In short order, I had him ready to go. "How long has your daughter been riding?" I asked the man.

"We did the program last summer, and Jenny loved it," he said. "She can't wait to get back on again. She's over there, in the blue sweatshirt." He pointed toward the observation deck, where a thin teenaged girl sat in a wheelchair. She smiled and waved. We waved back.

Tina came over to check Red's tack. "Put his halter back on over the bridle," she instructed me. "You'll lead him as Jenny rides. Try to let her do the work, but you be there just in case." "No problem," I thought. "I'm here, leading a horse again."

"Thank you for doing this for my daughter and these kids," said Jenny's father. "It means so much to them." He caught a tear with a swipe of his wrist.

"You're very welcome," I said. I wondered where he worked during the day to provide for his family, and what it must be like to come home to a handicapped child, to all the medical bills, to her total dependence.

Several horses were now lined up for the mounting block, and Charlotte lifted a boy into a saddle. Jenny beamed at Red as we approached. Her father helped her out of her wheelchair, and she stood unsteadily on her toes while she was outfitted with a wide blue belt around her waist. When it was Jenny's turn to get on, I held Red steady while Tina and Charlotte helped her into the saddle.

When I helped guide Jenny's foot into the sheepskin-lined stirrup, I realized how thin her legs were without the braces. My hand could almost encircle the calf of her leg, despite her thick sweatpants. Her toe pointed down and in. I looked up to see Tina uncurling Jenny's clenched hands to grasp the reins. Would this girl really be able to ride this horse? Her whole body wobbled unsteadily and I feared she would fall off.

Two more people came to Red's side and Tina gave some instructions that allayed my fears. "Kristen, you are in charge of the horse. Amy, you and John are going to hold onto the belt around Jenny's waist and walk beside the horse to make sure she doesn't fall off." Tina turned to Jenny. The helmet looked huge on her unsteady head, but beneath it was a joyous, crooked smile, so big it seemed wider than her ears. "Are you ready?" Tina asked.

"Oh, yes!" exclaimed Jenny.

"Off you go then," said Tina, and she turned to help the next rider onto the mounting block.

I looked up at Jenny. "Squeeze your legs and ask him to walk," I cued her. She did, and our team began to walk together on the soft dirt around the outside of the arena.

"Wheee!" cried Jenny. She smiled as she watched herself in the mirror next to the arena. We turned the corners marked by small orange cones.

"How old are you, Jenny?" I asked her.

"Fifteen, and my birthday is in two weeks!" she said.

"What do you want for your birthday?" I slowed a little to look back at her and felt Red's front hoof graze my shoe.

"I want a horse!" She reached forward a little and patted Red's mane.

"Me, too," I said. My heart felt as hollow as the Tin Man's chest. I thought, "You and I have something in common, Jenny. When I was fifteen, I had my first horse, and she was my life. She brought freedom to my life, just like Red brings freedom to yours. I miss having a horse so much."

"Pull on your outside rein," I said, and Jenny guided Red around the next cone. The teacher and riding instructor came out in me as I coached, cued, and encouraged her through the simple obstacle course. Every little success brought that big smile of joy to her face. Amy, John, and I continuously praised her efforts as she rode. Even Red, for his part, was as steady and patient as an old workhorse, and I loved him for that. He seemed to sense that he was carrying precious cargo.

Finally Tina called for the riders to stop and dismount at the mounting block. Jenny's cheeks were red and her grip on the reins limp from exertion. She continued smiling all the way into her father's arms. "You must be a teacher," said her father. "You really helped her along today."

"I'm trying to be," I said.

"Well, you're doing a great job," he said. Jenny hugged Red's neck. Charlotte took his saddle and handed me a brush and hoof pick. I smiled to myself as I took Red back to the center of the arena to groom him. Hope began to soothe and dim my feelings of despair.

A trickle of well-being flowed through me as I brushed Red's chestnut coat. The damp area under the saddle, the swirl on his forehead, the firm tendons beneath his knees and hocks . . . I'd never seen this horse before, but his body seemed completely familiar, as if he were some reincarnation of my old chestnut mare. I took my time getting the job done, enjoying the smooth feel of his coat and his horsey smell. I hadn't been so happy in months.

Tina finally beckoned me to load Red in the trailer to go back to his farm. I was reluctant to give him up and vowed to bring carrots for him. I would come next week and help, and all the weeks after that. As Tina tied Red in the trailer, I saw Jenny and her parents come out of the arena building. Jenny smiled and waved again. "Bye-bye!" Anyone would think we had been friends for years.

Although I felt a twang in my heart watching the horses go, I also felt it grow. I realized that life was not about complaining and wishing for more, and it certainly wasn't about trying to harm myself in a foolish attempt to escape disappointment. Life was about a teenage girl finding freedom on a horse, and all the people—the *important* people—who joined together to make that freedom possible. I waved once more and started back to my car, smiling and breathing deeply.

—Kristen B. Fowler

Under the Sign of the Red Horse

I got my real education under the protection of the Sign of the Red Horse, schooled by a half-quarter horse, half-Thoroughbred named Lance who was a lot older and wiser than me.

To understand this story, you have to know that this is the Wild West and accidents happen. On my fourth birthday in 1954, I wandered away from our western Washington farmhouse, across the shining field toward the dark of the cedar forest.

My grandfather's two-man logging rig squatted in a clearing between pasture and trees, raising up a saw blade like a dangerous head twice my size. I managed to tumble off the back of the seat onto the sharp teeth.

The blow stopped my face from growing. I had the chin, jaws, and cheekbones of a four-year-old during all those impressionable, sensitive, growing-up years. My coordination was poor as a result of the fall, too—"a quarter bubble off plumb," as my dad would say.

But the real damage was done at school. We had moved to a home by the Wenatchee River, east of the Washington Cascades, between apple orchards and the sage steppes. Bus number 15 came down the long hill of Horse Lake Road to the most distant stop to pick up us Brown kids first. A couple miles later, Perry Hobson got on at Western Avenue.

Perry started in on me in third grade and didn't let up until we both graduated from high school. His taunts were cruel and relentless. "Hey, No Chin. Who hit you with the ugly stick? What happened to your face? Looks like you fell on a buzz saw." He was a mindless bully, the first to claw open that suppurating lesion of the heart that most girls grow up with—the oozing pus that is fear of men, the raw flesh that is insecurity, the inflamed edges that are always trying to heal yet keep getting lashed open, fresh and bleeding, in the schoolyard.

I hid in the classroom from boys like Perry. I hated the blood-ied knees, the dirt on my pretty dresses, the feel of filthy shoving hands on my bare arms. And Perry always shouted, "Go home, Butt Ugly!" Still, Mrs. Blumhagen gave me a gentle push. "Go outside, Sandy. Play tetherball."

I stood in line, dreading the moment I would have to step up in front of the other kids. Finally, I tossed the tetherball in the air, brought my fist around to slam it, and wrapped the chain four times around my wrist. In the sour rain of laughter, I clawed frantically to free my arm from the chain. For the rest of the hour, I hid in a bathroom stall with my face in my hands.

On the bus ride home, Perry liked to stand up just as the bus jerked to a halt, pretending the movement of the bus made him fall on me. A swipe of his arm made sure I had to scramble under the seats to collect my books.

One day I got the idea I could get off bus number 15 before Perry's stop. It was a mile-long walk home through orchards. I took off my school shoes, tied them together, and slung them over my shoulder. Soft, dry clay puffed up between my toes. I was far away from Perry's jeering laughter, but another voice brought me up short. "What're you doing out here by yourself, Bucktooth?" Perry wasn't the only bully in the neighborhood. The Childress boy was seven years older than me, a misshapen lump of a teenager my father pegged as "two bricks shy of a load." He had a jackknife, and now he tossed it swiftly at my bare foot. The blade flipped in the air and slipped between my toes into the clay.

"Come on, Bucktooth. I'll show you mine if you show me yours." One hand fondled his zipper. I ran. He stumbled after me. The jackknife made the softest hiss as it passed through the hair by my ear. In my head echoed the schoolyard yells, "No chin!" and "Butt ugly!" Fear controlled me. It seemed that I would always be bleeding from that heart wound I had no words to describe or power to mend.

Life changed when Lance came to live with us. It was as if some new constellation had appeared in the sky over our river house. We called our imaginary pattern of stars the Sign of the Red Horse, but Red Horse School was more like it. Lance's first order of business as resident horse was to get my older sister, Cheryl, through high school. When she graduated and I began to tangle with eighth grade, Lance and I became constant after-school companions.

Lance was a handsome bay, seventeen hands high, burnished red with a roached black mane and flowing tail. Each of his front hooves was white to mid-cannon. A white stripe and soft black muzzle set off red-brown eyes that spoke a full emotional vocabulary. Play and adventure were his two favorite pastimes.

At fourteen, I was a large, big-breasted girl who hid behind my locker door in gym class and stood with my head down in the over-revealing gym clothes. The other girls stared at my out-sized chest and made rude remarks. I was always last to be cho-sen for teams. The situation on bus number 15 never changed. If it wasn't Perry, it was another bully shouting, "Fatty, Fatty, two-by-four, can't get through the bathroom door!" By the time I got home every day, I was churning with despair.

Lance spent his mornings grazing, but when bus number 15 came down the hill he began prancing in anticipation. He met me at the gate, tossing his head up and down, barely holding still long enough for me to get the bridle buckled behind his ears. I rode bareback with a light Western curb bit and a pair of old, soft leather reins. Riding felt like floating on a surging swell of muscle and tide.

We raced up the canyon past the bus stop, veering off to lunge up forty-five-degree slopes between sagebrush and balsamroot sunflower. High up in the hills, I'd slip off Lance's sweaty body and lean against his big chest while he cropped at the dry cheat grass. Gradually his heartbeat slowed, and my breathing steadied. I'd put my arms around his neck and place my bare feet on top of his two front hooves. When he lifted a hoof and took a step forward, I'd move with him. My heart pulsed with his great heart, and the startled bird of my fearful thoughts found a quiet roost.

When Lance had me settled down, he'd pull his head up and look at me. *Let's go*, he was saying. Sometimes he decided where we would go, and sometimes it seemed like I did. In some way, we had become one mind as we ranged over the steppes and buttes of our personal West until the red carnelian sun dropped behind those mountains called the Enchantments. We returned home in time to see the first stars come out. "Those stars are the Sign of the Red Horse," I explained as I brushed Lance down, "named especially for you." He tossed his head with a slab of hay in his teeth, spraying a half circle of alfalfa around us.

One day the gym teachers decided that the boys and girls together should play a game called "sockem." Red-faced, I couldn't focus with the boys staring at my breasts. Running and screaming kids kept several balls in play. I started to panic like a mustang filly caught in a roundup. When I heard someone yell my name, I turned just as a high-speed ball hit my right eye. Eyes bandaged, I was in the hospital for ten days. During that week, alone with my own apprehension and dread, I spiraled into a black depression.

As soon as I got home from the hospital, I retreated to the back of the pasture, where I burrowed into the grass and clay like an injured dog. Lance grazed nearby, rolling an occasional eye in my direction. On the third day, he came over and nibbled my neck with his rubbery lips. His long tongue licked all around the bandage on my eye. He blew on my unkempt hair, then shoved my arm with the side of his head. *Let's go!*

Listless, I mounted from the fence rail. We splashed across the river at Sunnyslope and an hour later we were at the confluence of the Wenatchee and mighty Columbia Rivers. The slow, dark animal movement of the water mesmerized me. I got this idea in my head that if we could swim the half-mile to the other side we could keep riding forever.

It was a dangerous fantasy. Here, the Columbia was forty-five feet deep. Its powerful current flowed downstream to the Rock Island Dam at five miles an hour. But I wanted to be in that deep water. I wanted to be pulled far away from the turbine of my own heart.

Lance went into the water willingly. We were both hot, and the cool water was delicious. I urged him out deeper until the sand bar dropped away. I hung onto the wet reins and floated above him. In fact, I floated above both of us. I was out of my body, my disassociation almost complete. From far above, I saw us swimming; I saw the distance behind and the distance before us. Then we passed the protective curve of slack water and entered the straight line of the current. The undertow felt like a giant eel wrapping its writhing power around our legs, dragging us downstream. I didn't understand what was happening, but Lance knew immediately—big water, big current, big danger. Flattening his expressive ears, he turned around and cycled his big hooves against the wrestling tentacles that were trying to pull him down toward the dam. I was still unaware of our danger.

Lance reached the sand bar and splashed quickly back to shore. I slid off while he shook himself vigorously, stinging me with hard droplets. Then he turned and looked me directly in the eye. With a snap, I was focused and brought to account. I heard his message in my soul: *Look at yourself. What's the matter with you?* No one ever spoke to me so clearly and directly before or after that moment, but no one has ever had to. My depression had to be addressed. I looked into the calm, dark lake of Lance's pupils, and my face reflected back our deep communication: *You must rise above the darkness, Sandy. Your heart must now beat slow and steady and true. You are half human, half horse, and it's time for your horse half to balance the human. You can rise above the mindless nips and bites of the unruly colts in your herd. Find a way, but never again try anything this foolhardy and purely dangerous.*

Then, as in so many other times, I cried, my head against Lance's red chest, my arms around his neck. He tolerated this, munching grass for a while, but then he gave me a shove. *Knock it off now. Let's go.* I got on, and we ran until the thundering drum of his hooves brought us home.

Lance stopped me from choosing a dark fate that day and every day thereafter. High in the air on his back, I was closer to the stars and farther away from cruelty. At Lance's school, I learned to pay attention. I learned to think and dream at the pace of a walk. I learned that two hearts pressed close and running as one can outrace painful words. Just this morning, decades after my last ride on Lance, I awoke with the memory of his breath on my cheek.

—Sandy Jensen

Honey

Every little girl deserves a guardian angel. A palo-mino mare proved to be mine. Today people talk openly about animal intuition, but in 1960, when my father placed me on Honey's back and sent us into the woods alone, no one thought of her as anything more than a sweet, gentle horse.

My mother suffered three heart attacks before she turned forty. The second one left her bedridden. Mom's life depended on taking nitroglycerin tablets several times a day. That meant she required full-time care so Dad could return to work at his barbershop. There were no visiting nurses or home health aides in Payson, Arizona, in 1960. And there were no other children or extended family to call upon. No one questioned my absence from school or the necessity of my assuming such a grownup role. So, at the tender age of seven, I became her caretaker and full-time nurse. Usually Mom asked for a pill when she needed it. But if she lost consciousness, her life depended on me, and my parents schooled me carefully in what to do and in what order. During this frightening and difficult time, a customer of my father's gave me a very special gift. He introduced me to Honey.

Like most little girls, I loved the idea of owning my own horse. Tom, who owned the local stable, visited Dad every week for a haircut. He was also my customer when I opened my shoeshine stand in the barbershop during school breaks. I would polish his boots, and he would entertain me with fascinating stories about his horses. I begged my father for riding lessons.

Eventually Dad gave in to my pleas. A "just one time" visit to the stable led to the rental of two horses almost every weekend. Dad loved horses, too, and rode well. But he and Tom could barely contain their surprise the first time they put me on Honey's back. I heard them tell Mom that I rode like I was born in a saddle.

Tom was a wise old horse-savvy cowboy who knew a match when he saw one. He told Dad to let me come to the stable whenever I wanted. Honey was not only the biggest horse in the stable; she was the favorite of every child in town. But Tom said he always knew when I was on the way, because Honey stood at the gate and waited for me. He told everyone who saw us together that there was something special between us. Honey loved kids, but this was different. Tom didn't have to understand. He respected his horses deeply, and told Dad he wouldn't charge me to ride when the stable wasn't busy.

Later, as an adult, I understood that Tom had found a kind way to let me ride without embarrassing my father. I'm sure he knew we couldn't afford the weekly rental fees, but the grizzled old cowboy apparently read people well, too. My dad wouldn't have accepted charity, even to make me happy, but he was doing Tom and Honey a favor, so that was all right.

Visiting Honey became the highlight of my day. We disappeared into the woods every day after school, until after the weekend my mother had her third heart attack.

It happened in the car on our way home from a picnic. I remember sliding off the back seat of the car onto the floor when Dad skidded to a stop on the gravel in front of the doctor's office. It was Saturday, but the doctor lived behind his office. Dad told me to wait in the car, jumped out, picked my mother up in his arms, and ran into the office without even knocking.

I wasn't a child who got upset easily, but my heart dropped into my stomach. We never went to a doctor without an appointment, and I knew Dad could barely lift Mother. He never carried her. And I was never left behind—I was an only child. Right before my fifth birthday I'd seen my mother in the intensive care unit of the hospital for the first time. This had to be bad. Very bad.

The news about Mom's condition spread through the community like wildfire. Tom came by that same weekend to issue an open invitation: Honey was mine, whenever I wanted to ride. This time the offer was nothing more than a gift for a frightened little girl.

After heart attack number three, nursing and homework filled my days. I sat in Mom's bedroom doing my schoolwork, handing out pills, and worrying each time she fell asleep. Every day when Dad came home from work, I ran out the door and headed for the stable.

Long rides through the woods on Honey provided my only relief from the swift journey into adulthood and the weight of responsibility. Sometimes I rode bareback. Other times, Tom saddled her for me. She listened to me with the patience of a wise old lady, and she licked my tears when I cried. She ran like the wind when I wanted to run.

When we rode out alone, it wasn't important for me to know my way. Honey always knew her way home. She also knew my riding skill better than I did. If I coaxed her to do too much, she simply refused, and nothing could make her change her mind. She also brought me home on time every day. Like most stable horses, she knew the dinner schedule and unerringly dropped me into Tom's arms on her way to the barn.

For many months Honey provided her special brand of therapy. Her constant presence, her physical size, and her warmth gave me strength and comfort. During our rides through the woods, I could relax and be a child. We explored nature and shared after-school snacks. Honey listened to me laugh, cry, and play. Not once did I question receiving advice and reassurance from a large, blonde horse.

Eventually my mother recovered, and Dad sold his barbershop to take a better job in the city. Tom offered to sell Honey to us, but the upkeep of a horse cost more than our family could afford, even without a mountain of medical bills. So Honey and I shared one last picnic. There were no tears; we both knew it was time to part.

Honey stayed with Tom and fulfilled her destiny. She lived out her days in the mountains and pine trees, helping other children, while I moved away to grow up. Her job with me was done. My journey through life was just beginning.

—Penny J. Leisch

Full Circle

At *age seventeen,* few times are more exciting than the weeks just before graduation, especially when the senior prom is only days away and you hold an acceptance letter from the college of your choice. But this seventeen-year-old could top all that: my parents had just arranged for me to take my horse with me to college. My Irish Thoroughbred, Taree, and I had been a team for many years. Together we had won high-point junior hunter in Arizona. Now as I prepared to attend Purdue University in Indiana, we continued to compete and ride in fox hunts.

A friend and I decided to celebrate these exciting times by driving from Arizona to a concert in Michigan. On the drive home, some oncoming headlights temporarily blinded my friend, and she lost control of the car. It rolled downhill several times before it came to a stop. A passing truck driver tried to put out the fire in the engine. He asked me if I could move; I couldn't, so I remained pinned in the car until the ambulance arrived.

The surgeons did what they could for my spinal cord injury, but I was paralyzed from the waist down. After weeks in intensive care, I was transferred to a rehabilitation hospital in Denver. Four months later, confined to a wheelchair, I returned home to try and re-establish my life. My parents sold my horse, my father retired from the Air Force, and my family moved to Houston.

Even while I surveyed the path to my future, I had to deal with my past. Very reluctantly I got rid of my tack, and a big part of my childhood. I missed Taree terribly. Not only had he been a big part of my everyday life, he had also been my best friend. My horse had played an integral role in shaping my secrets, hopes, and dreams. To this day, I feel deeply the pain the parting caused me. But even more I regret the pain it must have caused my horse, since I had been unable to say goodbye to him.

During the next several years, I enrolled in college, eventually accumulating three degrees while working full-time. I became a certified public accountant, married my husband, Ed, and we had a daughter, Katherine.

Katherine proved to be the catalyst for change in my future. At eight, she begged for riding lessons. While acknowledging the expense, I didn't put up much of a fight. For me, being around horses again, even at a distance, was the kind of heaven only horse enthusiasts can appreciate. Nothing can duplicate the smell of the barn! When I wheeled into the stable that first time after so many years, the odor immediately brought back a flood of memories and emotion.

At first I was cautious around the horses, and several of them were nervous around my wheelchair. I left the grooming and tacking directions to the instructor and just sat back as an observer. Even when Katherine started jumping, I kept my memories and experiences to myself. It was bittersweet to have to watch from a wheelchair.

After Katherine had been riding for a while, we decided to lease a horse so she could practice more often. We found one that was owned by a volunteer at a local therapeutic riding center called SIRE. Although I'd been disabled for twenty years, I'd never heard of this form of therapy for mentally or physically challenged individuals. I was instantly enthralled at the idea of riding again in a safe program designed for people with my abilities. I called the center the next day and signed up for lessons.

In June 2000, I started on a twenty-something-year-old mare with Olympic dressage competitions to her credit. It took a while to regain my balance, muscles, and confidence, but I persevered. I was thrilled to be back on a horse! In my second semester of classes, I learned that dressage had just become a Paralympic sport. My competitive nature kicked in, and my confidence started to escalate.

At the same time, I started on a new horse named Oiler. Both Oiler and I were veteran hunter/jumper competitors, so we learned the sport of dressage together. With the help of our instructor, we worked on increasingly complicated moves, such as leg yielding, serpentines, and shoulder-in. Not only was I doing all this with just the use of my upper body, but at the same time I was teaching a horse that had never performed dressage. Soon we started competing at local shows.

There were no other disabled riders in this part of the country, so I went up against able-bodied riders in regular dressage competitions. On the day of our first show, the wind chill hovered at twenty-three degrees. I piled on every piece of thermal clothing I had and off we went. As I warmed up with all the other riders I realized that, thanks to Oiler, we were all equal here. I smiled so much during my test that my lips froze to my teeth.

Encouraged by this experience, I decided to aim for the Paralympics. I competed at regional and then national horse shows and clinics to obtain the required elements and scores. In order to make either the national or international team, I had to earn good scores in a large number of recognized shows. Two scores for each of the three tests had to be submitted to the lists for the teams: the team test, the championship test, and the freestyle test. Only the top few riders would be considered.

During 2002, Oiler and I competed in many shows together, always with the support of SIRE and its staff. The head instructor, Karen, traveled with me on her own time, and the president, Molly, supported me in every way possible.

The competition was tough. During one show in April, the wind blew at thirty to forty miles per hour. Right before I was to go into the arena a huge branch broke off a tree near us and landed with a great splash in the lake. The normally laid-back Oiler spooked, and off I fell. Thinking I had only pulled some leg muscles, I got back on and competed in my three classes. Oiler was flawless, as usual, but he seemed unusually cautious. It felt as though he knew something I didn't. I had some trouble moving him into a working trot instead of a jog, but chalked it up to my own fatigue and the excitement of the spill. When I dismounted, my leg was broken. The injury grounded me for four months.

In September I started riding again, but I only had until the end of October to get in shape and earn the rest of the necessary qualifying scores. Everyone was sympathetic and tried to reassure me, "There's always next year." Well, no, there wasn't, if I wanted to make the 2004 Paralympics in Athens. By this time, Oiler and I were a team, and we could read each other perfectly. My cues to him were subtle, but he picked them up without fail. I knew we had a real chance.

In mid-November we learned our scores were good enough to get us on the international list. The next June we were invited to compete at the United States Equestrian Team "Festival of Champions" in Gladstone, New Jersey, the qualifying show to make the United States Disabled World Team. A good showing there would let me compete in the World Dressage Championships in September in Belgium.

The show corresponded with the region's rainiest period in the past hundred years, and the arena was outdoors. Accustomed to the desert climate of Arizona, I had never ridden in the rain. Not only was the arena flooding, but the route from our barn to the arena was a very steep, very muddy incline. Not for the first time, I put my trust in Oiler—to get up that hill, perform in the soggy arena, *and* get the scores we needed. To ride a horse that you know and trust completely at this level of competition creates a sense of confidence like no other. Once we made it up that hill, I knew we could accomplish anything. With water dripping off my visor, Oiler and I stepped through the little rivulets and lakes and on to the ride of our lives. When we were finished, he knew that he had performed well, and indeed he had, for we made the team. It is an incredible moment to know that you will represent the United States in an international competition. In Belgium, our team placed fifth overall and earned four spots on the United States Paralympic Team in Athens.

Today I have a new instructor, Jayne, and a new horse, Sir Lancelot. We are working to make the team that will compete in Beijing in 2008. My life has come full circle, with horses once again at the center of my hopes and dreams, albeit in ways I could never have imagined when I was seventeen. My experience has come full circle, too, as I bring my knowledge of therapeutic riding to the world. While not everyone can—or even wants to—compete as I do, there is much to be gained from being around horses. They offer limitless friendship and unconditional love, but most especially they offer freedom to both able-bodied and challenged riders alike.

Oiler's story has come full circle, too. For a twenty-three-year-old horse to give so much of himself and end his career with a win is a testament to his generosity and heart. I know that he did it for me. The year after our performance in Belgium, Oiler retired from SIRE. What else could I do but adopt him?

—Cynthia Ruiz

Contributors

Nancy Alexander ("Escape") is a freelance writer who rides all day and writes all night. Nancy lives in the Midwest with her daughter and Thoroughbred horse and says her goal in life is to be healthy enough in body, mind, and soul to ride until she's eighty.

Sue Pearson Atkinson ("In the Silence") has worked for thirty years as a broadcast journalist and is currently an independent producer of nationally distributed public television programs. Sue and her neurologist husband, Rick, raised five children and taught them all to ride, but none of them developed her passion for horses. In her friendship with a foster child, Sue has found her horse-crazy little girl, and Sue looks forward to many years of sharing her obsession with all things equine.

Wendy Beth Baker ("Trail Mix") holds a B.A. in English from Michigan State University and a diploma in book publishing from New York University. She has edited manuscripts for Doubleday & Co., HarperCollins, and Random House. After moving to Los Angeles, Wendy worked as editorial director of children's books at Price Stern Sloan and later as editorial manager of the book and audio division of the Walt Disney Company. Her original stories include "The Brightest Star," narrated by James Earl Jones. Her first nonfiction book, *Healing Power of Horses: Lessons from the Lakota Indians,* has sold nearly 10,000 copies. Her short story "Something about Mollie" appears in *Horse Crazy: Women and the Horses They Love* (Adams Media). She and her dog, cat, and turtle live in Burbank, California, where she is a lead editor at Yahoo Search Marketing. She spends most of her free time with Mollie.

Dede Beasley, M.Ed., L.P.C., ("The Promise") is a licensed professional counselor who has been in private practice for over fifteen years. Dede has developed equine-assisted psychotherapy programs for residential treatment programs, facilitates workshops and training at her farm outside of Nashville, Tennessee, and speaks at professional conferences about the application of her body/mind/spirit paradigm to the practice of equine assisted psychotherapy. She can be reached at *ponypeople@earthlink.net.*

Tami Bova ("Belle") trains horses in Elbert, Colorado, where she lives with her husband Brad, sons Chance and Blake, and baby daughter Cheyenne. Tami majored in equine sciences at Colorado State University and has been riding since she was seven years old. Belle had her third foal in 2006.

Judi A. Brown ("My Therapist") began riding with the local Pony Club at age eight. Later she rode hunt seat at local horse shows and fox hunted in the winter. After a fifteen-year hiatus from riding to attend college, work, and travel, Judi bought a Thoroughbred, hired an instructor, and became an accomplished event competitor. Today she keeps Virgil exercised and rides for pleasure.

Linda Karen Dicmanis ("Choosing to Lose") was born across the road from a racecourse, so had no choice but to be horse-mad from birth. Linda is the award-winning author of the fantasy *Horse Lords* series, with part of the proceeds donated to Brooke Hospital for Animals. For more information, go to *www.senfaren.com.* In her spare time, Linda competes on her two horses, Hobbs and BJ, or paints pictures of her equine friends. She lives in the Blue Mountains, Sydney, Australia.

Janet Eckles ("He Cried My Tears") is an inspirational speaker and writer whose work has been featured in regional and national magazines. She is the author of *Trials of Today, Treasures for Tomorrow: Overcoming Adversities in Life.* Find a daily dose of inspiration and uplifting stories on Janet's Web site at *www.janeckles.com.*

Kristen B. Fowler ("How Jenny Can Ride") began drawing and writing about horses at age six, although she never touched a real horse until age thirteen, when her parents gave her English riding lessons as a Christmas gift. Kristen has been involved with horses ever since: riding, showing, training, teaching at riding camp, volunteering with Horsemen for the Handicapped, reading horse stories to her elementary school students, and writing horse stories for readers of all levels. She lives in Ohio with her husband and two young daughters, who are begging for a horse of their own.

Elisabeth (Lisa) A. Freeman ("Learning to Laugh Again") is an award-winning writer from Michigan who has published over one hundred stories and articles and four books. Her recently released *Run for Your Life* is a thriller about her life as a teenage runaway. One of Lisa's stories, "A New Home," appears in *Chicken Soup for the Dog Lover's Soul*. Currently she is transforming herself from writer to inspirational speaker. For more information, go to her Web site at *http://lisafreeman.org*.

Joanne M. Friedman ("The Rat") has spent more than forty years around horses. She owns and operates Gallant Hope Farm in northwest New Jersey. A veteran English teacher and freelance writer, Joanne is the author of *It's a Horse's Life! Advice and Observations for the Humans Who Choose to Share It.*

Mary Hadley ("Some Things I Won't Give Up") grew up on the beach in San Diego, California, where she developed a great fondness for animals and rode horses. She married a cowboy, raised seven children on an isolated ranch in Nevada, ranched timber in Oregon, and later lived on a cattle and horse ranch southwest of Sundance, Wyoming. Later in life, Mary found time to write down her stories. She is a member of the Society of Children's Book Writers. Her work has been published in *Arthritis Today* and *Woven on the Wind: Women Write About Friendship in the Sagebrush West.*

Harmony Marie Harrison ("The Strength to Return") is a writer living in Oregon. She spends huge amounts of time riding, grooming, mucking, and distributing carrots, and is actively seeking her first horse. You may find Harmony wherever beginner-friendly horses are being sold.

Heather Hoffman ("My Pal") is Level I certified in equine assisted psychotherapy by the Equine Assisted Growth and Learning Association and a Registered Level therapeutic riding instructor through NARHA. She has a master's degree in counselor education and counseling psychology and a graduate certificate in holistic healthcare. She is a therapist at a nonprofit agency in Kalamazoo, Michigan, and works to raise awareness in her community about equine assisted activities. One day she hopes to work full-time in this special field, touching lives with horses. She is grateful for the wonderful friends and family in her life, including her partner, Jeremy, and their two dogs.

Susan Hutchinson ("Finding My Prince Charming") has lived most of her life in Seattle, Washington. She earned a degree in business management and worked in the finance industry until she took early retirement in 2003. Susan enjoys writing poetry and spending time outdoors, particularly horseback riding and playing with her dog, Cinder.

Sharla Rae Jahnke ("Our Horse of Peace") graduated from the University of Wisconsin-Oshkosh with a bachelor's in social work and now helps abused and neglected children. She has a black belt in Kuk Sool Won, a Korean martial art. Sharla lives outside of Atlanta, Georgia, with her husband, Tim, and their younger son. She is working on her first novel about growing up with a paranoid schizophrenic mother.

Sandy Jensen ("Under the Sign of the Red Horse") is a native of Wenatchee, Washington, who now lives in Eugene, Oregon. She is the author of a 2006 book of poetry, *I Saw Us in a Painting* (*www.walking birdpress.com*). Currently, Sandy is working on *A Horse Named Trouble,* a novel about a young woman and a black mustang. You may contact her at *chickadeeacres@yahoo.com.* After civilizing four unruly children, Lance, the horse in her story, retired to a long and happy life in the green pastures of the Skagit Valley.

Myra Langley Johnson ("My Special Olympians") has written for numerous publications over the past twenty years, including *Highlights for Children, Children's Writer, Today's Christian Woman,* and *Christ in Our Home.* She and her husband became therapeutic riding volunteers in 1998 and are avid supporters of the program. A midlife equestrian and dressage student, she rides as often as possible.

Sandy Keefe ("Getting to Know Blackie") is a nurse, freelance writer, and mother of three children, Burleigh, Shannon, and Allie. Today, Allie is fourteen and continues to ride at UCP Saddle Pals Therapeutic Center in Orangevale, California. The whole family volunteers at the center to support therapeutic horseback riding because it has made such a tremendous difference in Allie's life.

Penny J. Leisch ("Honey") is a full-time freelance writer who has twenty years' experience with special needs animals and rescued pets. As a certified holistic health practitioner, she writes newspaper and magazine articles, product and book reviews, essays, and pet education materials. Penny's work also appears in *A Cup of Comfort for Mothers and Sons* (Adams). Penny's Pens & Pics (*www.pennyleisch. com*), her resource Web site for writers, won a bronze World Wide Web Award in 2004.

Deborah Lewin ("My Opportunity") had never ridden a horse before beginning therapeutic riding at Equest Therapeutic Horsemanship in 1997, where she learned to turn her greatest challenges into her greatest opportunities. Now on the board of Equest, Deborah is a national ParaEquestrian athlete and has received both the NARHA Independent Rider of the Year Award and the Equest Levi Strauss Award. She has been featured in many newspapers, magazines, and television specials, and is included in the made-for-television documentary *Fear to Faith: Ordinary People, Extraordinary Lives,* scheduled to air in 2006. When sharing her motivational stories with audiences, she encourages everyone to "Ride strong through the journey of life."

Jan Mader ("Beautiful Silence") is a children's book author who lives in Columbus, Ohio, with her husband, Chuck. They have three wonderful sons and two grandchildren. Jan's newest book, *Tango and Tilly,* is based on the antics of one of her own delightful horses.

Jody McPheeters ("Competitive Spirit") is a mother and retired CEO living in Northern California. She is spending her "golden years" gardening, writing, cooking, and enjoying life with her three grown children, her golden retriever, Cody, rescue dog, Ikea, and twenty-pound cat, Jake. Her good friend Melanie adopted Borage, who has a happy, healthful life in Phoenix, Oregon, where Jody visits him regularly.

Charlotte Mendel ("Grass Can Get Greener") lives in Nova Scotia. She has published articles in *City Lights,* the Tel Aviv supplement of *The Jerusalem Post,* and *The Weekly Press* (Nova Scotia). Charlotte's novel *Unlike the Great Majority* won an Honorable Mention in the 28th Annual Atlantic Writing Competition for unpublished manuscripts. Her stories have appeared in *The Nashwaak Review, The Shore Magazine,* and *Horse Crazy: Women and the Horses They Love* (Adams). She has two young children and has been heard to mutter,

"I should have stuck with horses." Poteet lived to the ripe old age of thirty-one.

Katherine Mooney ("Kayla and Music") grew up in New Orleans and learned to ride shortly after she learned to walk. She remembers high school as a dim blur of going from barn to barn, riding, volunteering, and teaching lessons. Katherine recently graduated from Amherst College and will stay in New England for graduate school. She still makes time to do as much stable work as she can.

Barbara O'Connor ("No Longer Seeking Sandpipers") has been involved with horses since she was ten and has owned and loved many horses. She is a professional dog trainer. Barbara and her husband live in southern Oregon with four horses, seven dogs, three cats, and three goats.

Rebecca Paradies ("Cutter, Peppy, and Me") is an expressive arts therapy graduate of the European Graduate School in Sass Fee, Switzerland. She is an accomplished artist and combines her skills in the arts with spending time with her horses. She lives in Tucson, Arizona, with her daughter, a small herd of animals, and her two horses, Cutter and Peppy. She is happiest at the barn working with clients and witnessing amazing personal transformations.

Dawn Prince-Hughes, Ph.D., (Foreword) is adjunct professor of anthropology at Western Washington University. In 2000, she was diagnosed with Asperger's syndrome. Her lifelong connection with animals—particularly horses, dogs, and gorillas—proved essential in her journey from struggling with symptoms to seeing her innate sensitivities as gifts. Dawn shares this powerful transformation in her national bestseller, *Songs of the Gorilla Nation: My Journey through Autism.*

Cynthia Ruiz (Introduction and "Full Circle") manages her own certified public accounting firm in Houston, Texas, where she lives with her husband and daughter. She was an accomplished hunter/jumper rider as a teenager, and Cynthia currently competes in dressage. She represented the United States in Belgium at the World Dressage Championships for ParaEquestrians. As a current member of the board of trustees for the North American Riding for the Handicapped Association, she is focused on educating the world about the many incredible benefits of equestrian activities.

Linda Seger ("One Horse, Two Transformations") lives and practices riding to music in Colorado. She is a theologian, teacher, and author as well as horseback rider. She holds a bachelor's degree in English, master's degrees from Immaculate Heart College Center in Los Angeles and the Pacific School of Religion, and a Th.D. from the Graduate Theological Union. Her books include *Jesus Rode a Donkey (Adams)*.

Ellen Bain Smith ("One July Night") is a former French and English teacher who turned writer of creative nonfiction and fiction. Her latest cause is teaching creative writing at a juvenile detention facility in Virginia. Ellen wishes she could teach her students riding as well.

Paul A. Spiers, Ph.D., ("Chanson de Roland") is an assistant professor in the Behavioral Neurosciences Program at the Boston University School of Medicine and is affiliated with the Clinical Research Center of the Massachusetts Institute of Technology. At seventeen he worked as a mounted ranch hand at a trail ride farm near Montreal, Quebec. After moving to the Boston area, he learned to play polo and began riding to hounds, eventually earning his colors as a whipper-in. He also competed in combined training at the novice level. In November 2005, he became president of the board of trustees of the North American Riding for the Handicapped Association.

Hilary C. T. Walker ("Kelly Comes Through") is British (which explains the excess of middle initials) and lives in Richmond, Virginia, with her American husband, Anglo-American son, a menagerie of dogs and cats, and four horses. In April 2005, the youngster, Cruz Bay, bucked her off at a local show in front of all her friends. After his mum, Kelly, suggested he cooperate with the hand that feeds him, he rallied and joined Kelly in winning a total of five one-day events to show her that he is just as special as Kelly. Hilary's friends have now stopped laughing at her.

Samantha Ducloux Waltz ("Yoga for Two") has published fiction and nonfiction under the names Samellyn Wood, Samantha Ducloux, and Samantha Ducloux Waltz. Her personal essays currently appear in a number of anthologies. She lives in Portland, Oregon, with her husband, a very large dog, and a very small cat. Her mare Vida lives nearby and gives her many quiet hours of pleasure in the arena and on the trail.

Lezah Yeoh ("Mitchell's Journey") lives in Fairfield, Connecticut, with her husband, Ian, and two sons, Mitchell and Mason. She is a fashion designer by trade and an avid photographer. Her greatest joy is watching her sons as they blossom. Mitchell, born with a genetic kidney disease that also affects his liver and spleen, is meeting life's challenges with courage and good cheer. His hobbies include music, art, computers, and, of course, horseback riding.

A. Bronwyn Llewellyn has enjoyed a long career in the museum profession, researching, writing, and editing scores of exhibits on such diverse topics as high technology, jazz, the civil rights movement, garbage, honeybees, the Vietnam War, skyscrapers, and ancient Chinese astronomy. She holds a *magna cum laude* bachelor's degree in English from William Jewell College in Missouri and a master's in museum studies from the Cooperstown Graduate Program in Upstate New York. Her books include *The Goddess at Home: Divine Interiors Inspired by Aphrodite, Artemis, Athena, Demeter, Hera, Hestia, and Persephone* (Rockport); *The Goddess Home Style Guide* (Rockport); *The Shakespeare Oracle* (Fair Winds Press); *Blooming Rooms: Decorating with Flowers and Floral Motifs, with* Meera Lester (Rockport); *Horse Crazy: Women and the Horses They Love* (Adams Media), and *The Everything® Career Tests Book,* with Robin B. Holt (Adams Media). She enjoys knitting, making handmade books, cards, and jewelry, and writing fiction and screenplays. The highlight of her week is Tuesday, which she spends with the exceptional horses and people at the National Center for Equine Facilitated Therapy in Woodside, California (*www.nceft.org*).